PRAISE FOR ALICE SINK'S WRITING

"Sink has taken her memories and channeled them into five years of research and writing that resulted in her...book *The Grit Behind the Miracle*, which chronicles the true story of the Infantile Paralysis Hospital that was built in 54 hours in 1944."
—Jill Doss-Raines, *Lexington Dispatch*

"Throughout the rare glimpses from 1900 to around the early 1950s, Sink stuck to one consistent theme in *Kernersville*. Sink portrayed...the sense of community."
—Brandon Keel, *Kernersville News*

"*Boarding House Reach* reminds us of one of the most important truths of life: There are no ordinary people! Every story here is fascinating—and every one importantly belongs to history."
—Fred Chappell

"Community abounds in a colorful new book about the history of North Carolina boarding houses—a traveler's guide to a lost place that was small-town and worldly at the same time."
—Lorraine Ahearn, *Greensboro News & Record.*

"A very highly recommended addition for academic and community library collections, *Boarding House Reach* could serve as a template for similar studies for other states."
—Midwest Book Review

"*Hidden History of the Piedmont Triad* recounts a number of interesting stories from throughout the Triad—from historic people and places to lesser-known colorful slices of life."
—Jimmy Tomlin, *High Point Enterprise*

"[In *Hidden History of the Piedmont Triad*] Sink writes about Lexington's downtown dime stores. She describes how each counter was like a different department of the store, with a candy counter and comic book sections popular with children...and makeup counters that carried old-fashioned items such as Tangee lipstick and Evening in Paris perfume."
—Vikki Broughton Hodges, the *Dispatch.*

Wicked
HIGH POINT

ALICE E. SINK

Charleston — London

THE
History
PRESS

Published by The History Press
Charleston, SC 29403
www.historypress.net

All images are courtesy of the Library of Congress.

Cover design by Karleigh Hambrick.

First published 2011

Manufactured in the United States

ISBN 978.1.60949.372.1

Library of Congress Cataloging-in-Publication Data

Sink, Alice E.
Wicked High Point / Alice E. Sink.
p. cm.
Includes bibliographical references.
ISBN 978-1-60949-372-1
1. Crime--North Carolina--High Point--History. 2. Violence--North Carolina--High Point-
-History. 3. Criminals--North Carolina--High Point--Biography. 4. High Point (N.C.)--
History. 5. High Point (N.C.)--Social conditions. 6. High Point (N.C.)--Moral conditions. 7.
High Point (N.C.)--Biography. I. Title.
HV6795.H48S56 2011
364.109756'62--dc23
2011024053

For Randi Johnson, good family friend—who, by the way, "does not have a wicked bone in her body."

Contents

CONTENTS

CONTENTS

Preface

I think it is extremely important to reconnect with the various dictionary definitions of "wicked." *Webster's New World Dictionary* (Second College edition), defines it as

> *morally bad or wrong: acting or done with evil intent; depraved; iniquitous; Generally bad, painful, unpleasant, etc. but without any moral considerations involved (a wicked blow on the head); Naughty in a playful way; mischievous; Slang: Showing great skill (he plays a wicked game of golf).*

High Point and its people have always been good to me. Family and friends live there. I taught writing courses for thirty years at High Point University. Today, I present programs and have book signings for High Point businesses and book and civic clubs. So, my personal perception of the city is positive; however, as is the case in all places, history does sometimes rear its wicked little head, and when it does, chilling—but true—stories are revealed.

Acknowledgements and Contributors

Once again, many thanks to my husband, Tom, who continues to offer suggestions and proofread my manuscripts. I truly appreciate my History Press editor, Jessica Berzon, who always kept me headed on the right track while I was researching and writing this book. Her editorial advice is priceless. Jaime Muehl, senior editor, kept me focused on Chicago (15th ed.), with some house deviations, and for this advice I am most grateful. Katie Parry, my publicist, works diligently to arrange presentations and book signings, and I sincerely appreciate her continued efforts and publicity. As for Jamie Brooke Barreto, sales specialist, let me assure you that her marketing skills are superior, and for that talent, I am grateful.

To all the High Point University Smith Library folks who helped me find necessary research materials through interlibrary loan and who helped me access places on the Internet that I never dreamed were there, thank you. David, Mike, Bob and Nita: you never ran away when you saw me entering the library! I appreciate the helpfulness and kindness of librarians at the High Point Public Library who assisted me with my research.

I also wish to acknowledge all those native High Point folks who gave me inspiration, ideas, tidbits and specifics concerning wicked High Point.

Finally, on another positive note, I want to thank all those High Point people who, through great efforts and sacrifices, helped "right many of the wrongs."

PART I
Now You Know

Nineteen-Year-Old Jailed for Series of Thefts

On or about October 26, 1944, James Otis Byrd, age nineteen, was jailed for a series of thefts at High Point homes. Here are the details, as reported:

> *James Otis Byrd…is being held in jail at High Point in default of bonds, aggregating $3.75 after police of that city stated he had confessed to entering five residences and stealing money and other valuables. The High Point police stated Tuesday they were investigating him also in connection with several other residential thefts, of which he denied knowledge. The housebreakings are reported to have all occurred during the week prior to Byrd's arrest.*
>
> *Byrd confessed to the High Point police the residences he invaded and the loot that he gathered from each home:*
>
> *Residence of Tom Lovings, 115 Taylor Street, leather bag, silver, clothing, shoes and other articles, valued at $25.*
>
> *Resident of Mrs. L.C. Martin, Highland Road, Rt., watch, knives, and other articles valued at $25 and several dollars in cash.*
>
> *Residence of Arthur Snider, 300 Oak Street, shotgun, shells, clothing and money—total value not yet estimated.*
>
> *Residence of C.B. Mallock, 105 Morris street, jewelry and cash valued at $25 or more.*

Along with Byrd, his friend, Perry Brewer, age forty-two, was also arrested and charged with impersonating a laundry deliveryman and entering the home of a sight-impaired man, as well as stealing a bag of laundry. Upon being questioned, Brewer said he was not a partner with Byrd.

BLACKMAIL CAN BE SWEET SORROW

In a July 28, 1909 newspaper account, it was reported that Miss Daisy Caudle of High Point, accused of blackmail, faced charges in federal court:

> *Miss Daisy Caudle of High Point faces the serious charge in the federal court, of attempting to blackmail a number of ministers of the Methodist Protestant church. She is charged with writing letters, threatening exposure unless certain sums of money were paid, to Rev. G.F. Milloway, of Winston-Salem, Rev. R.N. Melton, of Weaverville, Rev. T.M. Matthews, of Randleman, all Methodist Protestant ministers, and Rev. G.E. Biven, of the M.E. church of Randleman.*

Newspaper reports do not indicate the type or types of exposure employed in Miss Caudle's blackmail attempts.

ORGANIZATIONS WANT CHINESE STUDENT GONE

The date was March 4, 1914, and the following article appeared in a "From All Over the State" column, printed here in its entirety:

> *The Jr. O.C.A.M., the P.O.S. of A, the Daughters of Liberty, and other organizations of High Point are striving to have excluded from the High Point High School one Leau Leong, a Chinese boy 10 years old. The boy is wonderfully bright. It is alleged that when he entered he had mastered the First Reader, practically memorizing the whole of it within five hours and he has been "eating up" all sorts of knowledge since in the same whirlwind fashion. His case has been taken before the attorney general of the state and opinion will be expected daily.*

There are no subsequent newspaper reports that explain the outcome of the case; therefore, the "expected opinion" seems to be unpublished.

Unsolved 1950s Murder

According to *High Point Enterprise* staff writer Jimmy Tomlin, "Nearly 60 years ago, inside an old, abandoned house in High Point, poor Mary Mangum Hopkins suffered one of the city's most gruesome murders—a murder that was the talk of the town, and one that remains unsolved to this day."

Newspaper accounts give the story of "a woman found strangled to death with a silk stocking, identified as Mrs. Mary Hopkins, about 30, of Durham, a domestic." Following is an article published in neighboring Lexington's newspaper:

> *The nude, decomposed body was in a vacant house a block from the business district.*
>
> *Mrs. Evelyn Roach of High Point made the identification late yesterday, saying the woman had worked for her as a domestic for a few weeks and had left three weeks ago.*
>
> *Dr. W.W. Harvey, Guilford county coroner, said there was evidence the woman had been murdered by a "sadistic sexual pervert" because a piece of plaster mounding had been thrust into the body, piercing vital organs.*

Another article entitled "Nude Body of Unknown Woman Found in Empty High Point House" explores the mystery even more:

> *The discovery, first reported at 12:30 a.m., sent squads of detectives on a city-wide check of all reports of missing women filed with police during the past several weeks.*
>
> *The body was found in a debris-littered front room of an abandoned frame house one block from the city's main street. It was lying face up with a nylon stocking knotted about the throat.*
>
> *Cause of death was not immediately known, pending an autopsy this morning by Coroner W.W. Murphy of Greensboro.*
>
> *Held under a $500 bond as a material witness, meanwhile, was Thomas P. Trogden, a 53-year-old lumber yard laborer, who stated he found the body when he wandered into the house yesterday morning.*
>
> *Trogden said he had been drinking and was afraid to go to the police until later in the day. He went to headquarters late last night and reported the recovery. He was immediately jailed as a material witness pending further development of the crime.*

Capt. W.G. Johnson, chief of detectives, said all available plain-clothesmen would be assigned today to check missing person reports filed in an attempt to establish the identity of the body.

Clothes found under the rear of the house furnished no immediate clues, Capt. Johnson said. Found in a heap beneath the floor boards of the low structure were a handbag, a pair of shoes, a dress, a coat, a single stocking, underclothing, and a nightgown. None of these bore laundry marks or other types of identification, Capt. Johnson stated.

When *High Point Enterprise* reporter Jimmy Tomlin revisited this heinous—yet unsolved—July 29, 1951 murder case, his research produced more startling wickedness, which follows:

Hopkins' nude body was found lying face up on the floor, with a silk stocking knotted around her neck and a cloth belt, most likely from a woman's dress, fashioned into a slip-knot noose and drawn tight enough to dislocate her neck.

Moreover, a piece of ceiling molding—about 27 inches long and about 1½ inches in circumference—had been inserted into the woman's vaginal tract so forcefully that it passed through her liver and punctured her diaphragm and lower left lung. Only three inches of the stick remained on the outside of her body, according to the coroner.

In 1963, High Point police lieutenant John Staley spoke at length with *Enterprise* reporter Frank Warren about the case. According to Warren's confidential notes about that conversation—which were discovered in an *Enterprise* file pertaining to the Hopkins killing—Staley expressed the opinion that he knew who had killed Mary Hopkins.

According to the notes, one of the suspects failed a lie detector test in 1956, prompting the polygraph technician to tell Staley, "That is your man."

The officer also told Warren the suspect was "a sadistic sexual maniac" whose wife confided that the suspect "would get drunk, take her to old abandoned houses and have intercourse with her, then beat her and force her to let him commit sexual atrocities that injured her."

On the night of Hopkins's murder, the officer told Warren, the suspect picked up Hopkins at the Modern Grill and took her to the abandoned house on Willowbrook Street, where he had sex with her, then killed her and abused her dead body.

The Thursday, March 15, 1951 issue of the *Beacon* gave additional information in a front-page article entitled "Curtis Hopkins to be Grilled at

Death Scene." Apparently, police officers had a plan. They decided to take Curtis Hopkins, husband of the deceased, to the scene of the murder and "put him through a real examination. I believe we will have a 'break' in the murder mystery." It's likely that the officers' reasons for suspecting Curtis Hopkins resulted from their research, which proved the man was in High Point between February 14 and February 19. Mr. Hopkins, it seems, was released from Sandy Ridge prison camp on February 14, when he went to High Point. While in High Point, Hopkins spent two nights at the home of Captain Ruff Long, retired fireman, on Willowbrook Street.

Officers do not believe Tom Trogdon, the elderly man who found the body, was in any way connected to the murder; however, they placed him in jail as a material witness. His bond was set at $500.

The *Beacon* printed that a mistake was made when it was reported that Mr. Trogdon passed the police station twice before he got up enough nerve to go inside and report what he found in the abandoned house on Willowbrook Street. Chief Stoker clarified that error:

> *Trogdon visited a local Main Street store last Thursday morning and purchased there a bottle of bay rum. He drank some of the bay rum. He later went into an alley near the Willowbrook Street house where the body was found to take another drink of the bay rum but realizing the house was vacant, he went inside to do his drinking.*
>
> *When Trogdon entered the house, he saw the woman's body stretched out in a pile of paper, but first thought it was a store window model so he proceeded to take his drink of bay rum. When he had taken the drink he started to examine what he thought was a wax figure and found out, much to his surprise, that it was the body of a real woman and the body was very much decomposed.*
>
> *Then Mr. Trogdon, still drunk, went to a room he occupied on Redding Street. He awakened near the midnight hour and told a roommate what he had seen and it was the roommate who telephoned the police and told them about the body Mr. Trogdon had found.*

The final paragraph of the *Beacon* article focuses on Chief Stoker's assurance that the dead woman's husband would be questioned immediately.

Even today, Mary Hopkins's murder remains High Point's most gruesome unsolved murder and is the topic of conversation and mystery presentations.

ORIGIN OF TRAGIC FIRE UNKNOWN

The September 28, 1904 account of High Point Furniture Company's fire indicates that it was the work of an incendiary, as indicated by an article entitled "Furniture Factory Burned Entailing a Loss of More Than $30,000:

> *Fire at High Point Sunday night destroyed the warehouse and $20,000 worth of manufactured goods belonging to the High Point Furniture Company.*
>
> *The engine room of the plant was partially destroyed and two large dry kilns, together with a large amount of lumber, were also burned, swelling the total damage to over $80,000.*
>
> *The origin of the fire is unknown, but it is presumed to have been the work of an incendiary. The night watchman employed at the plant, accompanied by another employee, had gone the rounds just a few minutes before the blaze was discovered, a few minutes after seven o'clock, and at that time there was no evidence that anything was wrong. The plant of the furniture company is situated in the factory district and for awhile several surrounding factory buildings were endangered by the fierce flames and the showers of sparks which flew from the burning building. A large number of freight cars standing on the side-tracks, were saved by the timely arrival of a yard engine, which pulled them out of harm's way.*

Fortunately, High Point Furniture Company was insured; however, it was estimated that only about one-fourth of the property would be covered. Another concern of owners was the fact that this was the second time within several months that this same company had experienced losses by fire.

TARNISHED REPUTATION

Historian and author Robert Marks wrote the following words: "While it sought to clean up deteriorating neighborhoods, High Point also found the need to purge its police force." Here are the details supporting Marks's statement:

> *The department had acquired a tarnished reputation during the previous decade through numerous accusations of selective enforcement and brutality, particularly toward the city's minority race, and internal investigations were viewed with great skepticism. The May 1933 legalization of beer sales had, for the first time, allowed citizens to lawfully consume alcohol,*

but illegal liquor continued to attract popular attention. Eight years later, several officers found themselves accused of colluding with bootleggers and gamblers, leading to several demotions and firings.

It seems that several policemen allegedly took the confiscated beer for their personal use or perhaps for resale. Furthermore, the bootleggers accused police of "extreme brutality" as their liquor stashes were raided. Both allegations produced a black cloud on the High Point police force.

His Liquor Must Have Been Very Bad

Ninety-year-old J. Harper Johnston (High Point's oldest citizen at the time) gave the following interview to the *High Point Enterprise* on January 9, 1916:

Shortly after the time the railroad was put in operation, the year being 1859, the charter for the city was granted by the general assembly. While this instrument was in course of preparation, a man whose name cannot be recalled by Mr. Johnston came to the city and opened up a saloon. It was the only place of business of the kind that High Point ever knew and possibly, nay almost certainly, ever will know. No one knew from whence the man came or whither bound after a stay of just 24 hours, about 18 of which were spent in selling liquor to certain of the thirsty inhabitants. He opened up one morning in a hurriedly constructed "store" on what is now known as North Main Street, his place of business being a primitive shack composed of planks and sheeting somewhat after the nature and style of architecture of a "lean to."

Newspaper reports indicate that his business was brisk; after all, he was the first High Point "saloonist." Unfortunately, his booze caused many serious street fights. This disturbed the town's sober citizens, so they supposedly drew up a charter that would prohibit the sale of whiskey within their fair city. Consequently, it has been written that this was undoubtedly "the first town or city in the state to adopt a stringent prohibition measure." But before the measure could be approved, the man disappeared for good:

The prohibitionists of 1859 did not wait until after the assembly had granted the charter to attend to the local liquor situation for the barkeep, after doing business for about 18 hours, saw darkness descend upon and about him in High Point for the last time. The next day he was gone, had silently gathered up the small remaining portions of his stock in trade, hitched his horse to a dilapidated wagon and had moved on—evidently, for there is no proof as to whatever became of him.

WE HAVE NOT SNIFFED THE FOUL ACCUMULATIONS

In a newspaper report dated July 16, 1955, and entitled "A Tip to High Point," it seems that Davidson County had "one mess not of its own making that need[ed] to be cleaned up." According to the article, the High Point sewage plant located in Davidson County had not been maintained properly. Interestingly, the reporter who wrote the story admitted, "We have not gone to the scene to take a sniff, and the rains of the past few days must have fleshed off the foul accumulations." The conclusion of the piece urged corrective measures so the "mess" would not return.

FEMALE AUTOMOBILE THIEF

On December 27, 1950, a newspaper account carried the title "Girl Bride Here Held for High Point Auto Theft." The "girl" in question was seventeen-year-old Mrs. Norma Jean Wilson, who was arrested in Lexington and placed in jail at the request of High Point officers. Her bond was set at $5,000. Here's the story:

Mrs. Wilson is alleged to have taken part in a robbery of an automobile and $100 in cash last week, according to reports. She allegedly accompanied Robert Taylor, 21, of High Point when the property was reportedly stolen from Paul Smith, also of High Point. Police in High Point report a considerable amount of cash was found on Taylor when he was arrested. He is also being held in jail pending a $5,000 bond.

Mrs. Wilson had only $3.50 on her person when she was arrested. She said the money was a gift from her aunt, and she denied having any part in the alleged theft.

Mill Loopers Disgusted with Interracial Affair

The year was 1951, and the *Beacon*'s September 13 issue bore the following front-page caption: "Workers Disgusted at White Girl 'Making Love' with Negro Man." The site of the "love making" was one of High Point's leading hosiery mills. In fact, loopers in the mill had become so disgusted that they had been going to their superintendent with multiple complaints. When nothing was done, they contemplated striking in an effort "to clean up the situation." Their disgust was rooted in the following events:

> *Persons employed at this particular mill say the Negro man will visit the room where loopers work and there talk with a white woman in question for a considerable length of time. These people say the woman shows every sign of being very fond of the Negro man and the fondness is mutual.*
>
> *White people employed at the mill say they have become so interested in "breaking up" the affair between the Negro man and the white woman that they are going to take what action they deem necessary to "stop it" if their complaints are not given consideration by the mill management.*
>
> *It is also reported by white women at this mill that the Negro man in question has been seen to visit an apartment where the woman in question lives and has been known to stay in the apartment for as much as two hours.*

So, what did the white woman say about all this? When she suspected that her co-workers at the mill were denouncing her, she told them that the Negro came to her apartment to "wax [her] floors." The mill women did not believe the floor-waxing story.

The Pokey Couldn't Stand the Strain

Author's note: The term "drive-in" here refers to a municipal or industrial public parking lot, not a drive-in theater.

The introductory paragraph of a *Beacon* article entitled "Sex Thrives at Drive-Ins" begins with the words "Ah, Love Is So Sweet" and offers specific examples:

> *What goes on in the cars near the school house is a Sunday school picnic to what the grownups are doing in a number of High Point drive-in parking*

lots, and some of the worst is going on right in the middle of town, not three blocks from the police station.

Lurid stores of lovers' lanes have paled in insignificance in the light of account of the sex orgies which are taking place in and around a number of High Point drive-ins.

It seems the police were unable to deal with the situation because, they said, "if all the offenders who violate the prohibition law, and who are guilty of disorderly conduct were jailed, the pokey couldn't stand the strain." One veteran officer made the comment:

It used to be if you walked beside a parked car and shined a spotlight inside, some guy would jump straight through the roof and come down with an explanation as long as your arm. But now-a-days, they park right under a floodlight, and carry on worse than grandma would have in the privacy of her own bedroom.

The beer joints were referred to as "a haven of refuge compared to the average drive-in parking, particularly as the night wears on through the wee small hours and into the morning." Specific incidents were pointed to:

One officer says a young man and woman were involved in such amore that they did not notice that a crowd of people had gathered about the car to watch proceedings. Suddenly the man realized that he was being observed. Whereupon with great indignation, he roused himself and cried: "What the hell! Can't I have a little privacy?"

The conclusion of the newspaper article was a comment from the editor, who said, "If you doubt this story, the paper will be glad to supply the policeman's name, and he in turn will give you the principals in the cast."

PART II
Amazing and True

MINK FURS STREWN ALONG ROOF

The High Point United Press International (UPI) caption reads: "Number of Furs Taken Is Kept in Police File," and the report of this theft is definitely unique:

> *Detectives kept silent today on the number of furs taken during a weekend burglary at a swank woman's apparel shop.*
>
> *The only clue to the size of the burglary was seven mink fur pieces which were found strewn along the roof at Roxanne's. The burglars apparently dropped the furs, valued at more than $3,500 while leaving in a hurry.*
>
> *Officers said entry was gained through a window. The burglars also broke into seven cash registers before turning their attention to the fur department.*

Perhaps the thieves got away with this unique robbery because newspapers gave no further reports.

HE CLAIMS HE WAS KANGAROOED THROUGH COURT

On September 24, 1949, Claude E. Shackleford was charged with the August 12 rape of a ten-year-old girl. As the case neared jury trial, Judge Susie Sharp made the following ruling:

Judge Susie Sharp yesterday ruled as incompetent the testimony of a psychiatrist but allowed him to make a statement for the court record after the jury was taken from the court room. The psychiatrist, Dr. Fred Taylor, said he examined Shackleford three times following his arrest and found the man to have a psychopathic personality which did not affect his ability to know the nature and consequence of his acts.

In a newspaper article entitled "Jury Convicts Shackleford of Rape in Guilford," the news from the courtroom in High Point took a different twist.

Claude Shackleford, 33, today faced execution in the gas chamber for raping a 10-year-old High Point girl last Aug. 12.

An all-male Guilford county superior court jury convicted him of rape Saturday night. Judge Susie Sharp sentenced him to die on Nov. 25.

Shackleford received permission from the judge to say a few words after sentence.

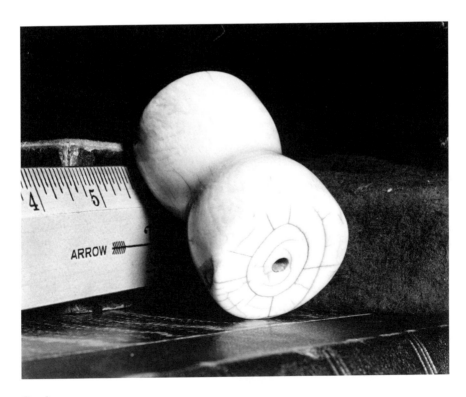

Gavel.

"First of all I think I've been kangarooed through court…I'd like to tell all the people in the courtroom I got a kangaroo trial."
Judge Sharp banged her gavel and said, "That's enough."

This newspaper report ended with the sentence: "Shackleford sat down beside his weeping mother." From all indications, Judge Sharpe had the last word!

"Unhappy" Valentine's Day News

While some February 14 newspaper accounts report on Valentine's parties and other happy occasions, a 1912 article entitled "Dan Hill Killed: Former Citizen of Midway Township Killed by His Own Son at High Point" reported:

Friends of the family in Davidson county will hear with regret of the very unfortunate tragedy at High Point Saturday night, February 3, in which Mr. Daniel Hill, a native of this county, who formerly lived near Midway church in Midway township, lost his life. For some reason the shooting was kept a secret for several days and it was not until Thursday that full particulars got in the papers. Mr. Hill died Wednesday night in a hospital at High Point.

When details of the killing were made available to the public, a newspaper report gave the following facts:

A horrible shooting affair that did not become generally known until yesterday occurred last Saturday night in High Point, and resulted in the death of Dan Hill, of that city, in a High Point hospital Wednesday night at 7:30 o'clock. Mr. Hill received the fatal wound at the hands of a son, who was quarrelling with a brother. The son admitted shooting his father, but said it was an accident, and seemed very penitent at the sad outcome. Both he and his brother are now in the High Point Prison, arrested on a warrant for murder sworn out by the High Point Chief of police.
The so-called accident is said to be the result of a quarrel between the two brothers, happening when the father intervened for the purpose of making peace. Whether the bullet was intended for the brother, or just went off in the tussle that ensued when the father attempted to make peace, is not known, and makes the case complicated. The real trouble is not known, and

there were only a few witnesses to the affair, whose minds do not seem to be clear on the real point of contention.

From other sources it is learned that the two boys, Numa and Bahnson, did not get along together well and frequently quarreled. They were fighting Saturday night, when their father tried to separate them and the fatal shot was fixed. Mr. Hill came of a fine family in this county and has many friends and relatives who mourn his untimely end.

While most Valentine Day events are joyous and involve love and kisses, this one would definitely make the "wicked" list.

DANGEROUS RAID OF BLACK PANTHER QUARTERS

Probably few High Point residents know of the February 10, 1971 Black Panther quarters raid by policemen. A UPI bulletin from High Point reveals specific details:

A police lieutenant was critically wounded today in an exchange of gunfire as about 60 law enforcement officers raided a Black Panther headquarters to enforce an eviction order.

Lt. Shaw Cooke, leader of one of the two city police platoons involved in the early-morning raid, was shot in the chest and rushed to a hospital for emergency surgery.

The law enforcement officers, outfitted with shotguns, flack vests and helmets, were reported to have fired volleys of tear gas into the one-story frame house before the shooting began.

A young Panther also was reported injured in the raid, but his condition was not believed serious. Authorities took four blacks who were inside the house into custody, including the wounded man.

The raid on the sandbagged house was conducted shortly after dawn and was timed to avoid the possibility that black youngsters would be at the home for a free breakfast program.

The house, located in a black area of the city, was reported sandbagged halfway up the walls on the inside and the windows were protected by steel bars.

The house had been rented by a "Mr. White" through a realty company.

Although the owner of the house requested that the Panthers be evicted, proceedings took a month. Still, the Panthers ultimately lost their appeal. It is interesting to note that today the Black Panthers and the policemen involved have reconciled through ongoing dialogue.

"Code of Silence" Among Gamblers

According to Paul B. Johnson, staff writer for the *High Point Enterprise*, who wrote an article entitled "Region Has Long History of Illegal Gambling," one truth is certain: "Law enforcement officers fought a painstaking battle against illegal gamblers as the lure of big-money payouts kept betting operations thriving." Obviously, High Point was no exception as many specific incidents have been recorded:

> *Often authorities were frustrated by the inability to make arrests in gambling-related felonies because of the so-called "code of silence" among gamblers, and because many feared retribution if they cooperated with investigators.*
>
> *Professional sports gambling was a popular center of attention in the 1970s and 1980s, as gamblers would buy tickets to bet on games.*
>
> *Hearings held before the High Point City Council in 1974 brought out allegations of widespread illegal gambling. A private home was linked to casino-style gambling that happened during weeks when the High Point Market drew tens of thousands of visitors to the city.*
>
> *In 1981, the manager of a former downtown High Point hotel was arrested and charged with allowing gambling in guest rooms.*
>
> *The gambling bust revealed that two hotel rooms contained poker chips, playing cards and cash. As High Point police officers and state Alcoholic Beverage Control authorities arrived to make the arrest, the manager supposedly called a hotel room from his office to warn gamblers of the impending bust.*

As time went by, gambling continued in High Point, often with a different "twist":

> *In 1982, a High Point couple and other associates were arrested and charged in a gambling operation cloaked in the cover of a nonprofit bingo business tied to a supposed missionary foundation. The nonprofit served as a way to cover up high-stakes gambling, authorities said at the time.*

The next year, High Point police made arrests after an undercover detective posed as a gambler at a city lounge. The detective indicated that he was offered winnings if he could achieve a certain number of points on an electronic poker machine. Also, in 1983, eight people were arrested for illegally operating video poker machines at a High Point pub.

One of the largest gambling busts happened in 1984 when more than 50 people were arrested and 23 gambling machines seized by High Point police. The arrests occurred after undercover officers from High Point, Greensboro and the N.C. Alcohol Law Enforcement Agency were approached at 17 city businesses by employees offering a chance at gambling games.

Two years later, High Point police raided a gambling house in the city. The officers seized gambling devices, betting sheets, a craps table, nearly $9,000 in cash and a stun gun.

In the late 1980s, High Point-area law enforcement officers seized $500,000 worth of gambling paraphernalia…after stopping the driver of a vehicle on Eastchester Drive. The bust occurred in early October just before the Major League Baseball playoffs, which was a peak time for gambling.

Consequently, according to research and Johnson's article, "Illegal gambling has a checkered, colorful—and too-often deadly—heritage in the region."

CHARGE OF CRIMINAL ASSAULT

In a February 4, 1925 newspaper article entitled "Davidson Jury Acquits Farmer in Assault Case," the following events allegedly happened while a sixteen-year-old girl's father was at work in High Point:

Everett Gordon…was found not guilty by a jury in superior court here Saturday afternoon on a charge of criminal assault proffered by his sixteen-year-old sister-in-law. Gordon was indicted by the grand jury on the capital charge but Judge McEloy charged the jury that it could return one or two lesser verdicts, assault with intent to rape or assault upon a female, or it might acquit. If there was consent on the part of the prosecuting witness, in the opinion of the jury, this would be ground for acquittal, the court stated. Gordon's wife, a sister of the chief prosecuting witness, sat with him throughout the trial while the younger girl sat with her mother. The father of the two women was at work in High Point while evidence was being heard Friday, it was testified. However, he is said not to have been a material witness.

Testimony from the sixteen-year-old girl, re-created the morning in question:

Miss Edith Albright, accuser of Gordon, testified that she was sixteen last June and a sister of Gordon's wife. On November 26 last, about eleven o'clock in the morning when Gordon, who lives only about 100 yards away, came to her home and asked to get some smoking tobacco from the small store near the Albright house kept by the witness' brother. Her father was employed in High Point, her mother had gone to that city and her brother was away from home temporarily, a state of facts she said ascertained by questioning her.

Miss Albright said she got the key and unlocked the store, secured the smoking tobacco and charged it to Gordon, who went toward home. In about five minutes he returned and said he wanted chewing tobacco also. Expressing doubt there was any in the store, she said she again unlocked the building but found no tobacco. Gordon came behind the counter where she was and looked under the counter for the tobacco, but agreed there was none there. He then seized her and carried her screaming and kicking to a small rear room of the store building where vegetables were kept, she testified. Her description was of an assault only partially completed.

The witness said she told Gordon she would have him arrested but that he replied that if she did he would swear against her. She told her mother of the incident when she returned home about an hour later, she said, and shortly accompanied the mother to Thomasville, where physicians and officers were consulted.

On cross-examination, Miss Albright testified without apparent confusion and apparently detracted nothing from her original story. Mrs. Albright corroborated her daughter's testimony as coinciding with what was related when she arrive home on the day in question.

This article was continued on page six; however, some old newspaper archives are unreadable, as was page six. We can only assume that the jury did not believe Miss Albright's story because Everett Gordon was acquitted.

MAN CRASHES AUTO OF CHIEF OF POLICE

If one is intoxicated and crashes into the chief of police's automobile, that's a wicked mistake. In an article entitled "Chair City Man Crashes Auto of High Point Chief," dated January 25, 1934, details were given concerning the wreck:

Sigman Wellborn, of Thomasville, was seriously cut about the face when the car he was driving struck a parked car belonging to Chief of Police W.G. Friddle in front of the chief's home on English street, High Point.

Wellborn, who according to investigating officers was intoxicated, ran into Chief Friddle's car, turning it completely around, clipping off a telephone pole and then turning over himself. Wellborn was pinned beneath his car.

He was carried for treatment to the Burrus Memorial Hospital in Sechrest's ambulance, where officers removed a bottle of liquor from one of his pockets.

Wellborn was charged with driving while under the influence and violation of the Prohibition law. He was released under a $500 bond.

STOLEN GOODS

A February 4, 1935 newspaper article entitled "Stolen Goods Are Recovered at High Point" gave a detailed account concerning "one of the largest quantities of stolen goods recovered here in months [which] had been seized by the High Point police department." Following is the complete story:

The police swooped down on a house at 711 Asheboro street, and from the information obtained there staged a second raid at 410 Park street, arrested W.H. Dickerson, 30, and sought Jones Dickerson, alias James Smith, a third brother, who escaped.

Officers from Davidson and Alamance counties, notified of the capture, arrived here and identified nearly $500 worth of the loot as goods having been reported to them as stolen, in recent months. More than half, however, remained unclaimed. Police believe that when the remainder is identified many of the robberies that have been perplexing city and county officials in this section will be cleared.

Among the loot recovered was a motorcycle stolen Monday from Ingram's Pharmacy, bicycles, a variety of automobile equipment, plumbing equipment, garage equipment, etc.

When a local plumber reported to police that he was approached and asked if he wanted to buy any or all of the plumbing equipment, the two brothers were arrested.

SUIT FOR DAMAGES OVER TELEGRAM

A November 26, 1902 newspaper account entitled "Mental Anguish Suit: The Western Union to be Sued for 'Bulling' a Message" gave a prime example of what can happen when one word is substituted for another:

The peculiar misconception and misreading of a message sent from the telegraph office at Salisbury by an operator of the Western Union on the line between there and High Point some time ago, gave rise to a heart-rendering scene at High Point, and a suit for damages will grow out of it. Messrs. Wescott Roberson, of High Point, and J.A. Barringer, of Greensboro, have the case in hand, and announce that suit will be brought against the Western Union, based on mental harassment growing out of negligence of the company. The amount of damages they will claim has not been given out. But the facts, as complaint will state, are substantially as follows:

On November 20th, Mr. S. Arthur Thompson, superintendent of the Central Manufacturing Co's chair plant at Lexington, was taken by his father-in-law, Mr. Lovelace, to the Whitsehead-Stokes Sanitarium in Salisbury to be operated on for appendicitis. The operation was performed on Nov. 21 and proved successful. The next day when the patient was out of danger, Mr. Lovelace filed in the telegraph office at Salisbury to his son at High Point, where Mrs. Thompson was with her mother, this message:

"Operation performed. Patient dying; will return him to-night." The word "doing" had been changed to "dying," "well," to "will" and "home" to "him."

Upon receipt of this intelligence Mrs. Thompson and her mother fainted, and the services of two physicians were necessary to restore them. Mrs. Thompson was uncontrollable, however, until it was promised that she could go to Salisbury. On the next train then nearly due. Quite a procession accompanied her and her mother to the train, both being beside themselves with grief and shock. Proceeding to Salisbury, Mrs. Thompson found her father "comfortably asleep," as his train for High Point was not due, and her husband resting quietly at the sanitarium, all danger from the operation being over.

Isn't it amazing how the misspelling of three little words can change the entire meaning of a message?

SELLING CIGARETTES TO MINORS

Apparently, in 1902, High Point merchants selling cigarettes to minors became a major problem—as indicated by the following February 5, 1902 newspaper article:

The cases against a number of High Point merchants for selling cigarettes to minors has been set for next term Guilford Superior Court. The law restricting the sale of cigarettes to minors has been much abused. We venture to say the boy who buys cigarettes is not asked one time in ten if he is over sixteen years of age.

CIVIL WAR WOUNDED

In his book *High Point: Reflections of the Past*, author Robert Marks writes about High Point during the later years of the Civil War, when the town "began to see the ugly side of war":

William Barbee had purchased the three-story brick hotel after the death of Jeremiah Piggott in late 1859. Governor Zebulon Vance agreed in 1863 to exempt Barbee from military service so long as he maintained his establishment as "an open house for wounded soldiers." In the early months of 1865 the conflict finally reached central North Carolina. After the battle of Bentonville, near Smithfield, an unprecedented stream of wounded poured into High Point, forcing the creation of makeshift hospitals in every possible location. It also brought another enemy, smallpox, forcing the operation of a "pest house" on the outskirts of town.

A Union military force arrived in High Point on April 10, 1865... The objective was to burn supplies, cut rail lines and destroy bridges behind the retreating Confederate armies. Colonel William J. Palmer's troopers burned the depot and several warehouses near the station. The fires threatened Barbee's "hospital," which was saved by pouring water over long cloths stretched across the eaves.

In his book, Marks refers to Laura Wesson as the heroine of the "pest house":

Though the war was officially ended within days, the hospitals of High Point remained full. The people of the town continued to minister to the sick and wounded. One such attendant was 19-year-old Laura Wesson…Knowing the risk of smallpox infection, she still chose to aid those forced to the "pest house."

The ending to this story is sad. Laura Wesson herself ultimately succumbed to smallpox.

SAFE-CRACKERS ARE FOILED

The question quickly arose among police: were two safe-crackings in High Point the work of professionals or just two local thieves who had started out on a safe-busting escapade?

Thieves were not able to "blow" the safe at the S.W. Horne Wholesale House, so they opened it by destroying the combination lock. They took $186—a considerable sum. However, the big stash was not in the safe but hidden in another place in the building. Fortunately, the robbers escaped with only the "safe" cash.

That same night, the thieves entered the Behr-Manning business and opened the safe there, escaping with only thirty or thirty-five dollars because they could not find the cash box.

Investigating officers believed the safe-crackings were the work of amateurs, even though professional thieves had been operating in the High Point area.

HIGH POINT'S FIRST HATCHET MURDER

The January 8, 1948 issue of the *Beacon* boasted tremendously large, bold headlines. "KILLS WIFE WITH HATCHET AND SLASHED OWN THROAT" certainly got readers' attention. The sub caption read: "Splits Wife's Head Open as She Tries to Escape Death." The opening paragraphs read as follows:

High Point's first hatchet murder in a generation happened here last night when W.W. Jones killed his wife by splitting her head open with a carpenter's hatchet and then stabbing her in the breast with an eight-inch kitchen knife to be sure she was dead.

The killer then went to his bedroom where he took a razor and slashed both sides of his throat and cut a deep gash in each leg—just back of the knee.

Then, according to the newspaper release, the Jones children—upon their six o'clock arrival at their 1507 North Hamilton Street home—found their father on the hall floor, bleeding profusely, and their mother at the bathroom door, dead in a pool of her own blood. They immediately called the police. According to the *Beacon*, dated January 8, 1948, Captains W.C. Johnson and W.G. Friddle arrive at the Hamilton home. They found the woman dead but Mr. Jones still breathing, despite the tremendous loss of blood he had suffered from his self-inflicted wounds.

An ambulance was summoned and Jones was transferred to a local hospital where late last night attending physicians said he would recover and that his wounds—while bad—were not critical.

A police guard was placed in the hospital with Jones for whom a warrant was issued last night charging him with the murder of his own wife.

Immediately after Jones was given first aid treatment officers visited the hospital and secured from him a confession which read as follows:

"I killed my wife. I used a hatchet and a knife and then I used a razor blade on myself. There was no one at home when I did it. I wanted to go, too. She wouldn't speak to me. She treated me awful. I asked her to call a doctor for me and she refused. We had lived together 31 years."

Jones blamed his children "because I couldn't work."

He added, "My wife would have been 56 years old her next birthday. She was in the kitchen when I first struck her with the hatchet."

According to the newspaper article, blood flowed freely in the Hamilton Street home. When Jones struck his wife the first blow in the kitchen, she ran to the front room with blood spurting from the hatchet wound in her head. Her husband, according to his own statement, followed her into the front room and struck her again. Then, Mrs. Jones, bleeding from two wounds to her head, started toward her bathroom, but her husband struck a third and final blow, which proved fatal. At that time, Mr. Jones took a razor and slashed both sides of his throat and both legs. His bloody footprints indicate that he walked around the house after he cut himself.

Mr. Jones readily admitted to the crime. It was reported that people who knew him for a long time said he was a dope user and a heavy drinker who stayed drunk much of the time. Officers said the hatchet-killer "had been a police problem for years." On one occasion, his family had sent him to a hospital for alcoholics; however, his treatment did him "no good and he continued to drink heavily and use dope when he returned home."

In the same issue of the *Beacon*, an article entitled "Reporters Not Allowed to Investigate Slaying," the editor wrote, "For the first time in the history of journalism news writers last night were barred by police from the scene of a murder and attempted suicide. That is something unheard of before in the newspaper profession." Representatives of the *Beacon*, the *High Point Enterprise*, the *Greensboro Daily News* and the *Winston-Salem Journal* were denied entrance to the 1507 North Hamilton Street home of the Jones family. The reason: "members of the family objected." Apparently, this was a "first" for Piedmont Triad reporters, and the following suggestion was made:

> *If that is going to be the policy of High Point's police department, then members of the city council, like in the big cities, should issue each and every news writer a police pass which entitles the news gatherer to enter police and fire lines.*
>
> *Such a pass has never been necessary in High Point, however, because the cops here are acquainted with all the newspapermen in the city and have, in the past, allowed news writers to look in on crime scenes so a descriptive story might be correctly written.*

WHERE WAS THE CHILD SUPPORT MONEY?

The January 8, 1948 issue of the *Beacon* ran a story, "Hubby Beat When Wife Tells Story," about Fred H. Lancaster, who appeared in court planning to prove his honesty and good intentions. He did not bring any receipts to prove that he had kept his promise to pay his estranged wife fifteen dollars a week for child support, so "that led to a court inquiry into what Fred had been doing with his cabbage."

Since the couple's separation, Mr. Lancaster said he had visited his wife's place of employment, spoken endearing terms to her, assured her he "wanted to do the right thing" and admitted he was "surprised she acted so cold."

When asked exactly what "right things" he had done, he could not point to any child support payments, as stipulated in the separation agreement. After hearing the case, the court decided on the following action:

> *By that time the court decided that Fred, in arguing his case, had made out a good case for his wife. That got Fred two years on the roads, all of it suspended upon the condition that Fred arrive in juvenile promptly each week and pay the required $15 on the line. The court advised him to visit his children only on such occasions as are reasonable and not to molest his wife at any time.*

Apparently, Fred felt he had been let off the hook because it is reported he "left the courtroom and breathed out numerous promises about what he intended to do."

WOMAN LEAPS FROM SEVENTH FLOOR

Mrs. Stella Ora Purcell, a popular High Point woman, fell to her death from a fire escape on the seventh floor of the Security Bank building. After jumping, Mrs. Purcell's twirling and twisting body landed on a Pontiac belonging to Silas B. Casey, prominent High Point attorney. Pedestrians on Commerce Street watched and screamed. Her death was ruled a suicide. Mrs. Purcell was said to have been despondent due to her poor health, and this was not the first time she tried to end her life. The following was reported in the July 31, 1947 edition of the *Beacon:*

> *Only a few months ago she slashed her wrists and throat in a suicide attempt, but after an extended stay in a local hospital, she recovered. Tuesday night the woman told a relative, "I had another washout tonight, but I will do the job tomorrow." The relative with whom the woman was talking at the time did not realize what she meant by the "washout" statement until yesterday morning when he was informed of her tragic death.*
>
> *Several months ago Mrs. Purcell underwent a major operation from which she had never fully recovered, and it is believed by her many close friends that her constant suffering caused her, to time [and] again, seek to end her life.*

According to an article entitled "Woman Leaps to Her Death from Top of Bank Building," Mrs. Purcell was a well-known High Point woman with many friends and customers of the beauty shop she owned and operated. Her first husband, Herbert Welch, had ended his life eighteen years earlier by shooting himself with a pistol. The popular cosmetologist remarried sometime after her first husband killed himself, but she and her second husband had not been living together for several months.

MISSING NEGRO WOMAN FOUND WITH WHITE MEN

Her name was missing from the newspaper report dated September 13, 1954, because, according to the news story, "authorities do not remember [it]"; however, the woman was described by officers investigating her disappearance as "nice looking."

> *Officers say the girl rode with her brother to the Rainbow Diner in a truck where her brother went for sandwiches. When the Negro man entered the Rainbow Diner, several soldiers loitering around in front of the place began to make remarks to the Negro girl. When the brother re-appeared at his truck, his sister was gone. He summoned Policeman Wade, who was on duty near the diner, and other officers were called to the scene to help with the investigation. Among the officers who aided in the hunt for the Negro girl was Sergeant Richardson.*

According to the article, the Rainbow Diner was often used as a meeting place. Soldiers who visited High Point knew they could go there at any hour of the day or night and find girls who were "willing to take a ride." Officers familiar with conditions in and around the Rainbow Diner said, "It's not safe for a nice girl to go in or by that corner alone late at night." So what happened to the girl?

> *Officers who investigated the girl's disappearance say she appeared at home, in the early morning hours, in company with the soldiers. The girl and the soldiers denied any wrong doings but officers are confident the Negro girl and the two white soldiers were not out after midnight just for the fun of staying out late. Since the trio, however, deny any wrong doing there is nothing police authorities can do about it.*

HOTBED OF PROSTITUTION

In the September 13, 1951 issue of the *Beacon*, the following caption appeared: "Police Call Clara Cox Project Vice 'Eyesore.'" The lead paragraph described the Clara Cox Homes as the "hotbed of prostitution in High Point." Detective W.C. Johnson related that the federal housing projects off Russell Street were a "sore spot we are almost powerless to erase, although Project officers are cooperating with the police in an effort to evict the undesirables who engage in illicit practices." Captain Johnson offered the following details concerning prostitution in the projects: "One of the real dangers are transient vice teams, usually made up of a man and a woman. They pass through, set up for business and move on very quickly." He added, "There is some permanent-type vice operation here." He said he was summoned to a house on Lindsay Street upon complaint of a housewife who said her husband had been lured into the nearby home by a woman engaged in "petty prostitution."

"We have evidence that this particular house has been and is being used for illicit purposes," the veteran officer declared. "Of course, we watch the place, but it is difficult—almost impossible—to support a prostitution charge unless the person or persons are caught in 'the transaction.'"

Captain Johnson also told the *Beacon* that some of the women living in the projects and using their homes as "houses of ill repute" were wives of servicemen who were away from home. These "wanton women tend to corrupt the whole picture," he said. It was Johnson's mission to eradicate prostitution all over High Point.

PART III
Front-Page Sensationalism

"Character" Killed on Streets

The newspaper caption on May 18, 1904, read, "Joe Jackson Killed. High Point Desperado Shot and Killed by the Chief of Police of That Town." These details followed:

> *Joe Jackson, a well-known character of High Point, was shot and instantly killed on the streets of that town yesterday afternoon by Chief of Police Gray. Jackson was drinking heavily. The Chief passed by him on the streets and Jackson cursed him. Later he attacked Officer Gray and attempted to take his pistol from him. A desperate struggle ensured, but the officer finally managed to get his pistol free and fired at Jackson. The first shot went wild, the second took effect in the stomach, and the third entered the head. Jackson was killed instantly.*

The final sentence of the article revealed Mr. Gray's statement concerning the shooting: "I regret it, but I had to do it."

Hit and Run, Manslaughter Charges Against Teacher

A December 23, 1948 newspaper report revealed that the High Point police charged a fifty-one-year-old teacher with hit and run and manslaughter in connection with the slaying of Mary Dell Pierce. The article paid brief attention to the accident and supplied extensive detailed information on the schoolteacher, Miss Lucille Dubose, who was arrested after the High Point police department sent out, over the radio, a description of the automobile:

> *The car was parked near where Miss DuBose lives. Two High Point police officers are in Thomasville this morning to return the vehicle here. Miss DuBose was released from police custody last night after she had posted bonds totaling $3,000. The manslaughter bond is $2,500 and the hit and run bond is $500.*
>
> *Miss DuBose, who teaches public school music and has about 500 Pilot pupils under her direction, was back at her school work this morning, it was learned. From an authentic source it was learned that she stated that if she hit anyone with her car in High Point Tuesday night she was wholly unaware of it. She had gone to the city, it was reported, to visit a niece, Mrs. Irvin Black, and had done some Christmas shopping. The three women who were hit were said to have been dressed in black and were walking along the street surface on their right at a spot not too well lighted.*
>
> *Miss DuBose is listed as a teacher at Pilot school, which is located in Davidson County near Thomasville. Miss DuBose, in addition to her work at Pilot has private classes in piano and art at Thomasville and is reputed to be an outstanding teacher. School officials said her moral reputation is impeccable. Miss DuBose, it is reported, becomes very much absorbed in her work. She wears glasses.*
>
> *Miss DuBose came to Pilot school this year from Morganton city schools, where she had been teaching, according to the record in the office of Supt. Paul F. Evans of the Davidson County schools. She has had about fifteen years of teaching experience, the record indicated. Her home address is given as Lamar, S.C., and her teaching address at 24 West Guilford street, Thomasville. She came to Pilot, it is said, with the finest of references.*

After a rather lengthy discussion of Miss DuBose's sterling personality and character, the newspaper article moved to specifics of the accident and the woman killed:

> *Probable cause was found today in the preliminary hearing of Miss Lucille DuBose, Thomasville school teacher, on charges of manslaughter and hit and run driving.*
>
> *The trio of women were carrying Christmas flowers and decorations to a church when the accident occurred.*

Guilford county coroner Dr. W.W. Harvey of Greensboro said death was caused by a broken neck. Police said the Pierce woman's body had been dragged 60 feet.

There was a report from High Point that the two injured women said they had exchanged words with occupants of a car which turned around and then struck them. It is reported here that Miss DuBose denies making any such turn as reported. A broken headlight in her car, an old model light vehicle, is said to have been replaced en route to school yesterday morning.

The woman killed in the accident Tuesday was walking along a busy thoroughfare here along with two other companions. They were slightly shaken up, but neither of the two was seriously injured. The women were Mrs. Iola Lunch and Mrs. Rose Jones, both of High Point.

It was just a few days later, on December 29, 1948, that Miss DuBose admitted to repairing her car, according to the following newspaper information:

She was bound over for trial at the January 18 term of court, at Guilford Superior court, High Point division.

Detective J.L. Kivett testified that Miss DuBose was arrested 24 hours after Miss Mary Bell Pierce was killed by an automobile December 21 while walking on a street here with two other women. The detectives said Miss DuBose at first had denied having repair work done to her automobile but that under questioning she admitted the repair work had been done. The 51-year-old defendant did not testify.

Interestingly, this was the last news on Miss DuBose and the outcome of the court case, so readers probably never knew what happened next.

KILLS MAN FOR HITTING HIS SISTER WITH CHAIR

In a rather unusual newspaper report, dated August 15, 1932, and captioned, "Raleigh Kaiser Shot to Death at High Point," the following specifics were given concerning a young man who had just moved to High Point and was slain at the home of a High Point woman:

Raleigh Julius Kaiser, 22…who yesterday is reported to have moved to High Point to live with relatives, was shot and killed there about eight o'clock last night by Melvin Mabe, 18, who is held on a charge of first degree murder, according to a press dispatch from High Point.

Mabe is quoted as freely admitting to the police that he shot Kaiser with a .38-calibre pistol after either Kaiser or an unidentified man companion had hit his sister, Mrs. Berta Shoe, with a chair at the apartment Mabe shared with Mrs. Shoe, his sister on North Main Street.

Police reported finding evidences of a struggle in the apartment, with a pack of shuffled cards and overturned pitcher. Mrs. Shoe was lying on a bed weeping, saying she had been struck with a chair. The pistol had only been fired once.

Kaiser after being shot ran from the apartment calling for an ambulance and fell almost in front of the Northside Baptist church. He died at the High Point hospital without regaining consciousness.

Mabe is quoted in a story from High Point that when he pulled the trigger Kaiser and a "little short" man were standing in the doorway of the Shoe apartment.

Early newspaper reports often covered shootings but neglected to follow through the next day or next week with updates.

THIS MAN KNEW LIQUOR SELLER; WOULDN'T TELL

Front-page newspaper reports in 1933 were written with honesty and, often, a bit of humor. Such was a December 7, 1933 article, which proved to be both honest and humorous:

S.G. Swaim actually bought a barrel of liquor from a man he knew, he told the court. But the frankness didn't do S.G. any good, for he stopped right there. Admitting he hadn't forgotten the fellow's name, Swaim said that he simply wouldn't tell.

"Thirty days," replied the court, but Swaim held firm to his determination in face of the sentence for contempt.

It seems, according to the court proceedings, that Swaim and his brother, Jerry Swaim, were both on trial for possessing liquor for sale. S.G. pleaded guilty to ownership of the forty gallons in a barrel that county officers dug out from underneath the henhouse of Jerry's home, where S.G. also resided. S.G. took the stand and said it was his liquor and that Jerry "had naught to do with it." That apparently did not satisfy the judge, "who was a bit skeptical about this story." He fined the two men accordingly:

> *He placed a fine of $100 each against the two Swaims and sentenced a road sentence upon condition that they not be found in the county. S.G. paid the fine and costs but Jerry gave notice of appeal to superior court and furnished bond to the February term.*

He Cut a High Caper and then Charged Cruelty to Camp Overseer

The May 30, 1906 newspaper account titled "Guilford Convict Shot" related how "four Negros and one white man" attempted to escape from the Guilford County chain gang. The article focused on James B. McMillan, alias Brent Amory, a young white man who forged checks and bonds—and "cut a high caper in the social circles." Here is the rest of the story.

McMillan was convicted and sent to the roads for two years. Before dying, he told his real name and said his people lived near Lexington, Kentucky. He was twenty-five years old and had evidently been well bred in a home of wealth and refinement. He stated that he had gotten into several scrapes and went to Greensboro, where he committed the folly of forgery. His mother was dead, but his father was living, and he earnestly asked that his people learn nothing of the disgrace that had befallen him.

Before his death, he not only revealed his heritage but also insisted he had been treated badly by the chain gang boss. He charged the boss with cruelty and stated he "could not have stayed there anyway."

This all seems a bit strange for a front-page newspaper report!

Hurt in Factory at Tender Age of Nine

The year was 1902. The title of the newspaper article was "Supreme Court Finds No Error. Interesting Statistics in Supreme Court Opinion." The subject was a nine-year-old boy who was injured at Alma Furniture Company in High Point:

> *The Supreme Court in its decision Saturday, Judge Clark writing the opinion, passed upon an interesting case touching child labor in factories.*

The opinion of the court in its concluding portion gives some most interesting statistics with regard to the child labor regulation in various parts of the world. This is a question of the day in North Carolina and this will be read with interest.

William Fitzgerald, by his best friend, sued the Alma Furniture Company of High Point, Guilford county for damages, and the jury awarded him $1,000. The case was originally tried at Davidson Superior court, Fitzgerald being a native of this county.

The boy was nine years old. One day when his father was absent he went to the factory to get work. He was given twenty five cents a day and his work was [on] a moulder [sic]. The next day he tailed the planer and the next day at 1 o'clock was put to work on the sander. He worked there an hour before he got hurt. While the man running the sander was away the boy testified that he leaned against the machine, did not think he was in danger, laid his hand on it and had his hand mashed.

Justice Clarke cites the statutes and opinions regulating the employment of children and says: "With this consensus of opinion in nearly the entire civilized world, it might be that it was negligence per se to put a child of the tender age of nine years to work on a dangerous machine, which he had never seen before, without any instructions or warning and to leave him there alone without stopping the machine."

The verdict? "The court finds no error."

ROBBERY AT THE SHERATON HOTEL

"Miss Porter Loses Valuable Coat in Hotel Robbery" was the intriguing caption for an August 5, 1929 newspaper article. The specifics follow:

Miss Frances Porter, formerly Miss Frances Briles of Thomasville who gained international notoriety several months ago when she was deported from Cuba after an alleged attack on a wealthy Atlanta man on whose yacht she had gone for a cruise, was the victim of a robbery at the Sheraton hotel at High Point during a big dance one night last week, according to the Enterprise.

Handsome evening wraps belonging to Miss Porter and to Miss Alice Barbee and Mrs. A.L. Green, of High Point were taken during the course of the dance, which attracted many guests from High Point and nearby

A society woman in a
fur coat.

*cities. Miss Porter's coat was an imported Japanese garment embroidered
with Japanese golden fox fur.*

*An unknown young woman is said to have been seen leaving the coat
room with several wraps but was not suspected at the time, it is said.*

The last sentence of the robbery report—"Miss Porter has appeared in
musical comedy productions and is regarded as an exceptionally skilled
dancer"—definitely changed the tone.

GUILTY AS CHARGED!

A front-page September 27, 1956 story began: "'Guilty as charged' was
the verdict of a Davidson County Superior Court Jury this morning in
the manslaughter trials of a 18-year-old High Point girl and a 44-year-old
Greensboro man." Details were as follows:

The charges grew out of the death of Billy Ray Pierce, 23, of High Point, last January on Highway 109 south of Thomasville. Patricia Upton received a two-to-four-year sentence, suspended for five years. Judge Leland McKeithen passed sentence about 12:30 this afternoon. The Upton girl was ordered to pay the costs, and to pay $500 for the benefit of Pierce's family. She is to remain under the State Probation Commission.

Strange, but there was not one word about the identity or sentencing of the forty-four-year-old man.

Boarders Walk Out

A September 24, 1955 front-page article entitled "Boarders Walk Out at High Point Mill" immediately raises the question: what's the job of boarders in a textile mill? The answer: boarders are workers who size and shape hosiery. Here is the rest of the story:

Boarders at Melrose Hosiery Mills are on strike. They also were the first ones to walk out two months ago, leading to a general strike, settled with a wage increase. Meanwhile, boarders at all unionized mills here are to take a strike vote tomorrow.

The next day's newspaper did not print the results of the strike vote.

Liquor? Or No Liquor?

The newspaper's front page carried the following article entitled "Liquor Vote Debated in High Point":

The High Point City Council is expected to sit as a committee of the whole tomorrow or Saturday to consider a petition for a city ABC liquor election.

A group of High Point businessmen petitioned the council earlier this week to ask the Guilford legislative delegation for an enabling bill to hold the election.

Church leaders were reported today to be gathering forces to oppose the proposed referendum.

An interesting observation concerns the fact that at the time of this report, beer and wine were legal in High Point; however, Greensboro was Guilford County's only city with an ABC liquor store.

Involuntary Manslaughter

A March 13, 1947 newspaper article entitled "High Point Man Pays for Death of Lexington Woman" read:

> *Guy D. Grimes, High Point citizen, will pay $3,250 to the estate of Ella Bradshaw, well known Lexington Negro woman who was fatally injured in an automobile wreck involving a car driven by Grimes at High Point last December.*
>
> *Grimes was charged with involuntary manslaughter in superior court at High Point and in the judgment entered there Monday, a sentence of from one to two years, was suspended on condition he make the compensatory payment noted above. His license to operate a motor vehicle was also revoked for two years.*

Investigation Was "Sneaky"

A January 5, 1950 newspaper account entitled "Ex-Corporal Crowell States Investigation Was 'Sneaky'" reveals some interesting facts concerning the firing of highway patrol corporal Johnny Crowell by Commander C.R. Tolar. Apparently, Crowell's dismissal came as quite a surprise after his fourteen-plus-year's service. Here is Crowell's story, as reported in the article:

> *"Sometime the middle of last week some friends of mine…reported a 'strange man' was asking questions about me. I did not realize what he could be asking but I started looking around," Crowell said.*
>
> *"I learned during the time the type car the man was driving and that it carried dealer plates. The questioning went on for a couple of days," he said.*
>
> *"Friday I spotted the car I believed to be driven by the man. It carried dealer plates and was a black Buick. I was on patrol at the time and stopped it for the purpose of a check of license just as I have on many occasions before when dealer plates are carried on strange cars that operate in my district," he said.*

The newspaper account then went on to tell of Crowell stopping the driver, who wore civilian clothes. He determined that the driver, who identified himself as George Oakley, was driving a state-owned car. Crowell said he told Oakley his name and asked if he had ever heard of him.

After Oakley left, Crowell checked the automobile license plates and discovered the car belonged to a High Point used car business—which was against the law, because state-owned cars are not supposed to operate on used car licenses.

Crowell learned that days had passed before Oakley filed his report, but Crowell had already been fired. He called the decision "rather sudden."

A follow-up January 7, 1950 article entitled "Scott Says Patrol Commander Is Doing Good Job: Governor Comments on Charges Made by John Crowell" defended Colonel Tolar:

> The governor made the comment at his news conference in reply to a reporter's request for comment on recent charges levied against Col. Tolar.
>
> The charges were made by John Crowell, a former Highway Patrol captain relieved of his duties last Saturday. He charged Tolar "is in the used car business" and owns at least two farms.
>
> The governor observed that some action should be taken if Tolar is spending too much time in private business. However, he said, "as far as I know, Tolar is doing a good job. I've always been able to get in touch with him at any time of the day or night."
>
> "I don't think he can be accused of not giving enough attention to his job," Scott added.
>
> Col. Tolar's only comment on Crowell's charges was the declaration that Crowell was "dismissed for failure to carry out orders and for inefficiency."

HUDDLED CLOSE IN THE CAR

On December 29, 1955, a *Beacon* article entitled "Police Jail White Man, Negro Girl Companion" reported on an arrest in the vicinity of Five Points. Patrolman E.D. Young and another officer riding with him followed the zigzagging car up Montlieu Avenue, stopping it in the vicinity of High Point College. Following is Young's statement:

> Young said a white man who gave his name as J.E. Sparks was driving the car and that Lenora Burris, 49-year-old Negro woman, was huddled close to the driver on the front seat of the car.

Sparks was charged with reckless driving and placed under $100 bond. Young said Sparks had been drinking but wasn't sufficiently intoxicated to be charged with drunken driving.

The Negro woman was charged with drunkenness and placed under $50 bond.

Interestingly, Sparks told Officer Young that the Burris woman was his maid and that he was taking her from Winston-Salem to her home in High Point. At the court hearing, Judge J.A. Myatt ruled that Sparks pay a fine of fifty dollars and court costs. The woman was taxed with ten dollars and costs.

PART IV
Believe It or Not

ALMOST BLIND, SO PARDONED

The June 14, 1905 High Point account of an unusual pardon is printed below:

> *The old man McFarland, who was convicted and sent to the roads for improper conduct with a girl under 15 years of age, has been pardoned. The old man had become almost blind, and his health was also wretched.*

On the chain gang.

PROHIBITION VIOLATION? OR NOT?

In a December 7, 1933 newspaper article, Judge John J. Hayes ruled that the Volstead Act was now inoperative. His logic was that "the Eighteenth Amendment was repealed without reservation when the Twenty-First Amendment was proclaimed." His explanation continued:

> *Since the Volstead Act and supplementary Federal legislation were passed by Congress solely under authority of the amendment they became inoperative when the amendment died, in the opinion of Judge Hayes.*
>
> *The ruling was made in cases charging prohibition law violation against Byron Gibson and Claude Chambers, charges that came up from Rockingham county. Gibson, by the way, was caught at High Point last week with a quantity of liquor and faces trial in a state court there.*

The Senate Judiciary Committee on the amendment of the Volstead Act.

Attorney X.I. Walser of High Point made the motion for dismissal of the charges and argued that the law under which it was proposed to try his clients is now ineffective. District Attorney J.R. McCrary argued for the government that the law was an active one at the time it was violated, regardless of the status after repeal.

At the conclusion of court that day, McCrary presented another argument. He said that if the defense were correct, then repeal of the Eighteenth Amendment "would open the prison doors for all now serving liquor sentences under the Volstead Act."

Demands Ransom in Rural Mailbox

The July 22, 1949 news release entitled "Streeton Murder Trial Continues, Witnesses Called" gave an account of court events:

Defense witnesses were called today to testify for Charles G. Streeton, 49, Jamestown short order cook who is accused of murder.

The state presented 17 witnesses yesterday in its attempt to convict Streeton of the slaying of Carl Davis, 29-year-old High Point cripple.

Davis, son of a High Point ice manufacturer, was shot to death last March 14. His bullet pieced body was not found until two days later after his family had received a ransom note demanding $5,000 for his safe return.

Among state witnesses were the parents of the slain man, Mr. and Mrs. McKinley Davis. Both wept while they told of events surrounding their son's death.

The elder Davis told of receiving the ransom note and said he placed a dummy package in a mail box on the Greensboro road as directed in the note.

High Point police, among them Defective Captain W.C. Highfill, testified that Streeton was arrested about two hours later as he placed a handkerchief-draped hand into one of the two mailboxes at the designated spot.

The prosecution closed its testimony during a session last night.

Short-order cook Charles G. Streeton, age forty-nine, faced life in prison for killing his crippled brother-in-law and sending the victim's parents a $5,000 ransom note. These details from High Point were explored the next day, on July 23, 1949, in a newspaper article that gave the following details:

Charles G. Streeton was convicted of first-degree murder Saturday by a Guilford county superior court jury which had heard six days of evidence and deliberated four hours and 25 minutes. The jury recommended life imprisonment. Judge George Patton of Franklin heeded the recommendation. The defense gave notice of appeal to the State supreme court.

Streeton was charged with slaying Carl Davis, 28, of High Point, last March 14. He was arrested near a rural mail box where he allegedly directed Davis' parents to put $5,000 if they wanted to see their son alive. High Point police said that after 18 hours of questioning Streeton led them to the bullet-pierced body of Davis under a bridge near High Point College.

The next sentence of the newspaper article definitely changed focus: "A woman, Mrs. Melvina Martin of High Point, was foreman of the jury." The concluding sentences again switched tone. They read, "Mrs. Streeton and Mrs. Davis burst into tears when the verdict was announced. Streeton and Davis were composed."

Fight at the Rainbow Diner

On Wednesday, July 12, 1950, a "bloody battle" took place late at night at the Rainbow Diner, located at North Main and English Streets. According to a newspaper report the next day:

Walter McDaniel was in the Rainbow Diner when he saw his wife enter the eating place with Theodore Krupezynsk and that without any exchange of words the husband seized a bottle and struck the man with his wife a terrific blow. The bottle broke and the man was badly cut about the head and face.

Then the two men stood off at arms length and began to "slug it out." They fought like tigers until the cops arrived to "break it up."

Officers had to take both cut and battered men to the hospital for stitches before they could be sent to jail.

A lemonade stand.

All Over a Glass of Lemonade

While many historic arguments or disagreements were about property ownership, jealousy or women, this one took a new and different approach, as recorded in the newspaper on May 8, 1907:

> *Two negroes employed by Lane Bros, near High Point fell out over a glass of lemonade and one pulled his ready gun, shooting Clifford Baxton in the arm. He then escaped although pursued by an officer accompanied by a bloodhound.*

All this trouble for a glass of lemonade?

Small Chance for Saving His Life

In a newspaper article dated November 23, 1904, specifics were related concerning a High Point accidental shooting, which took one man's eye. The details that follow are complete, but gruesome:

> *Near High Point this morning, George Gould of New York, while shooting at birds on his preserves accidentally shot an attendant, Edward Burns, of High Point. The shot struck Burns in the face, several entering the*

eye. Gould's special car was attached to an engine and the wounded man, accompanied by Mr. Gould, was brought to Greensboro where an eye specialist, after examination, stated that other wounds while painful are superficial, but there is small chance for saving the eye.

An eminent New York specialist said he would apply his skills and science in order to save Burns's eye.

Stricken by an Axe While in Bed

The January 1, 1904 newspaper's front-page captain read, "A Citizen Stricken by an Axe While in Bed—Much Feeling Aroused." We probably would snicker at the "much feeling aroused" placement if this were not such a wicked offense. Here is the story:

> *A burglar entered the home of Mr. Lewis Payne, of High Point, Thursday night, and while Mr. Payne was asleep struck him three times on the head with an axe, inflicting serious wounds. The burglar fled when Mrs. Payne awoke, leaving the bloody axe on the floor. Mr. Payne is the machinist for Snow Lumber Company, a steady, hard-working citizen, and much indignation is felt on account of this attack. At first it was thought that he could live, but this morning the physicians have hopes of his recovery.*
>
> *Early the same morning parties tried to effect [sic] an entrance to the home of Mrs. Carter and it was reported at the time that she had been choked into insensibility, but the report was ungrounded, according to parties living nearby.*
>
> *The people are alarmed over the matter and sleep with one eye open at night with weapons at close range, and these persistent burglars will, no doubt, yet run across the "wrong" person, who will lay them out in short order.*

Chicken Stealing

A newspaper article dated February 19, 1902, called George Walker's stealing "wholesale thieving." This is what reportedly happened:

> *Mr. W.S. Lovelace, chief of police of High Point, came down yesterday afternoon with a negro named George Walker, who was placed in jail to*

await the next criminal term of Guilford Superior Court having been bound over in a $100 bond by Justice J.W. Wilborn on the charge of stealing chickens. When arrested on the outskirt of High Point yesterday morning he had in his possession seven chickens which were stolen Tuesday night. Recently a large number of chickens have been missed both at High Point and Thomasville…and suspicion rested on Walker, but he managed to elude the officers until yesterday. Mr. Lovelace said that there was every reason to believe that Walker had swiped at least 300 in High Point and 150 in Thomasville—doing wholesale thieving, in other words.

Apparently, chicken stealing was an extremely profitable business in 1902.

THAT IS HIGH POINT'S BUSINESS

In the August 5, 1929 edition of the *Dispatch*, a journalist wrote a column entitled "High Point Police." The article, in its entirety, follows:

Something seems to be constitutionally wrong in the High Point police department but just what it is outsiders hardly know. And evidently High Point officials themselves have difficulty in diagnosis and prescription, for recurrences of disorder keep coming up.

Several changes in department heads have been made during the past two or three years. A number of patrolmen have been suspended or fired outright. One or more have been charged with being too handy with firearms, another officer was accused for leaving his desk and going out to work in the city election. He replied that he merely got "leave" to do this and got his pay from other than city funds for the period. There was a scandal about the disappearance of stolen loot from their police station to add to other accumulated worries. A police court official is alleged to be short in his accounts. Now another officer has been suspended because he kicked a youth in the stomach in the police station, where the latter had come to request a warrant for shooting a hole in his automobile. The desk sergeant refused the warrant, but it is indicated the matter wouldn't end there. The officer defends himself by saying that somebody told him that three boys who got into this complainant's car looked like three for whom the police were looking as suspicious characters.

Almost every police department now and then picks up an unworthy officer who brings shame to the office and handicaps the worthy policemen,

Policemen making an arrest.

who are the big majority. The whole cannot justly be condemned for the acts of individuals. But when disturbances become as chronic as they appear to be in the High Point department one is led to wonder if there isn't something wrong organically.

The article's conclusion softened a little, indicating that the police department's actions were "High Point's business" but should not affect all the people visiting or passing through the city.

SPANKING LEADS TO TRAGEDY

"Man Is Held In Death of Aged Mother" was the caption of a November 3, 1954 newspaper article. The story is tragic:

Ira Stiles, 49, of High Point faced a murder charge today in the death of his 67-year-old mother.
Mrs. Rosa Truitt Stiles died yesterday after she was kicked during a family argument while her invalid husband, Robert Lee Stiles, watched helplessly.

Spare the rod and spoil the child.

Police Lt. George Leverett said the argument started when Stiles objected to his sister, Mrs. Mildred Smith, spanking her grandchild. Mrs. Muriel Stiles Efird, another sister, said her mother intervened to keep Stiles from striking Mrs. Smith.

Leverett quoted Mrs. Smith as saying her mother was thrown down and Stiles kicked her twice while she lay on the floor.

What was Stiles's reaction to the above accusations? He admitted he had been drinking, and when he saw his sister spanking her child, he "flew into a rage." Then, when his mother fell across his leg, he pushed her to the floor.

MYSTERIOUS AND SEAMY SIDE

Jackie Hedstrom, supervisor of the Heritage Research Center at the High Point Public Library, researched the mysterious and seamy side of High Point for a presentation called "Lurid High Point: Tales of Murder, Mystery and Mayhem." Jimmy Tomlin of the *High Point Enterprise* wrote, "One story at a time, Jackie Hedstrom shines a glaring light on High Point's dark…side" and offered readers the following examples:

> *Consider, for example, the story of Veronica Cox, a waitress at the old Sheraton Hotel who shared an apartment with one of her co-workers and the co-worker's husband. One night in October 1954, Cox left work early after receiving a phone call; she was overheard telling the caller she's be ready in about 15 minutes. She went home and changed clothes—where she spoke briefly with her co-worker's husband—and then left, giving all indications that she would return and planned to work the next day.*
>
> *"The only thing she took with her was her sewing case," Hedstrom says. "Nobody saw who she left with, and she never returned. Her bank account was untouched, and police investigated all the names in her address book. There were reports of some prominent businessman in town for the furniture market who may have been a person of interest, but no one knew anything, so it's still just a strange disappearance."*
>
> *Another tale is that of Beulah Allen, a young woman who had moved in with a couple in the Fairfield community, Frank and Ermie Allen, as a servant of sorts. Beulah died on July 27, 1929, when she was scarcely 20 years old. Her death came as a shock to the community.*
>
> *"The speculation was that she had gotten pregnant and died from a botched abortion," Hedstrom says, adding that Frank Allen was rumored to be the one who impregnated her. The couple buried Beulah in the Springfield Friends Cemetery, adorning her tombstone with a tall angel—an unusual gesture, considering Quakers' tombstones were typically unpretentious.*

A few years later, Frank Allen committed suicide in the Springfield Friends Cemetery, and this action possibly made him Cox's murderer in the eyes of High Pointers.

CHILD LABOR IN MILLS

High Point's Pickett Cotton Mill, in existence from 1899 to 1933, was reorganized in 1910 and produced what was called "broad print cloths and other cotton goods." According to the book *Like a Family: The Marking of a Southern Cotton Mill World*, child labor was more the rule than the exception:

Child labor involved more, however, than the exploitation of youth. There were stories behind the expressions captured on film by Lewis Hine, stories that fit neither the rationalizations of mill owners not the fears of reformers. Mill work was a source of pride as well as pain, of fun as much as suffering; and children made choices, however hedged about by their parents' authority and their bosses' power.

Actually, at a very early age, children were taken to the mill with their mothers, as indicated in the following excerpt:

For mill children, life was paced from the outset by the ringing of the factory bell. Working women, who often had to return to their jobs within a few weeks of childbirth, adapted the nursing schedule to breaks in the workday...If labor was scarce, a woman who had neither relatives nor older children at home might take her baby to the mill.

As children got older, the mill was like a magnet, attracting their youthful curiosity and, all too soon, their labor. Until the 1920s no barbed wire fences, locked gates, or bricked-in windows separated the factory from the village. Children could easily wander in and out of the mill, and their first "work" might be indistinguishable from play.

Most children first learned about factory labor when they tagged along with a parent or sibling, carried hot meals to the mill at dinnertime, or stopped by after school. But this casual contact had serious consequences, for on such visits relatives began teaching children the skills they would need when they were old enough for jobs of their own.

While watching their parents work at various mill tasks, they quickly learned to operate different machines:

Mill managers expected children to master their jobs within a set length of time, usually about six weeks. During that period children worked for free or for a token wage...Almost all workers recalled proudly their ability to learn their jobs despite their youth...Children learned quickly because more entry-level jobs required more dexterity than technical know-how. It took a while to be proficient, but most children could learn the rudiments of spinning, spooling, or doffing in a few weeks.

The drunk.

CRAZY DRUNK ON DRUGGED LIQUOR

More wicked High Point escapades were recorded in a November 26, 1902 newspaper column entitled "Crazy Drunk, He Burned $500." This is what happened:

> *Joe Mitchell a hard working employee of the Piedmont Table Company of High Point, became crazy drunk Saturday night as the result of two drinks of corn whiskey, and demolished all the furniture in his house and burned up a trunk containing $500, the result of seven years hard work.*

This brief account concluded with the assumption that the liquor had been drugged.

THE "HIGH POINT LOCKOUT"

The title means exactly what it states, as explained by author Robert Marks in his book *High Point: Reflections of the Past*:

> *Until 1905, the town's workers and the factory owners had mostly seen eye to eye. J.J. Fariss had reported in 1903 that "the labor problem" which had affected the major industrial centers of the nation, in High Point was "not a problem." But as a result of union organizations that began the previous year, 1906 brought the city its own labor dispute, dubbed the "High Point Lockout" by journalists across the state. Manufacturers claimed it resulted from "out side influence" and "agitators…recently come to High Point," while union leaders believed the "rights of the people" were being "filched from them." It began on March 24, 1906, when the owners of 30 factories announced the firing of anyone wishing to remain in the unions. Though roughly one-half of the town's plants were involved, none were closed, and owners claimed "the quitting of the Union men will amount to nothing."*

The "High Point Lockout" involved approximately three weeks of negotiations before workers returned to their jobs.

DON'T DARE USE MY PERSONAL TOILETRY

Most citizens know that Noah Jarrell was the successful owner of the Hunt Hotel, located at the corner of High Point's Main and Commerce Streets. During the Civil War, locals took their sterling silver to the Hunt Hotel and hid these valuables in the Hunt Hotel's foundation. This story continues to be retold, even to this day:

> *The Jarrell family still talks of the day General Sherman's troops stopped at the Hunt for water. One of the Union officers picked up Mrs. Jarrell's comb and proceeded to brush his hair. Upon asking him if he was finished and receiving a nod, she promptly threw the brush in the fireplace. Fortunately the Northern troops left without further incident.*

Apparently Mrs. Jarrell felt she had experienced a terrible injustice and chose to burn the evidence.

TWO WEEKS EVERY SPRING AND FALL

A truly believe-it-or-not article entitled "Prostitution Legalized in High Point" appeared in the weekly magazine *Yes!*, which claims to be the "Triad's Alternative Newsweekly." Reporter Fakir Hassamadupis's column exploded on the front page of the January 4, 2009 edition:

The morning after the night before.

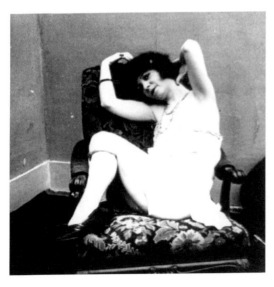

A scantily clad woman seated in a chair.

Daunted by declining industry, rising crime rates and the attendant stresses on its police force, increasing joblessness and an overall economic outlook, High Point officials last week passed emergency legislation that legalized the world's oldest profession—for four months out of the year. The High Point City Council voted 6–3 to repeal the state's longstanding law making prostitution illegal, with one caveat. The law only goes into effect during the biannual High Point International Furniture Market, which occurs for two weeks every spring and fall. "To be honest, the Las Vegas Furniture Market was just killing us," says the market's newly appointed director of vice, Tralfax Tarkanian. "I mean, who's going to go out to Vegas, stay in a casino, hit the clubs, have a nice buffet, maybe play a little craps." His eyes glazed over at the prospect.

"Anyway," he said, "we had to do something." The idea came up, he said, during a brainstorming session.

"Someone said, 'Man you can even get prostitutes in Las Vegas! It's totally legal!" the director of vice remembers. "But then we did a little research and it turns out prostitution is not legal in the city of Las Vegas itself. You gotta go out into the desert, where all the whorehouses—excuse me, I mean gentlemen 'spas'—are at. So, you know now we've got one thing Vegas doesn't."

The discovery prompted the market directors to move fast, and they successfully lobbied council to back the passage of this bill, where prostitution-related revenue, ranging from aggressive lap dances and "happy ending" style massages to full-fledged balloon rides.

A lady of the night.

Revenues are estimated at $1.3 million for each two-week market period. "The math is simple," Tarkanian said. "If you have 150 prostitutes, man it adds up." Area prostitutes seemed unaware of the new legislation.

"Anything you say, baby," said Chokana Wood, who was seen walking on Clinton Avenue singing the lyrics to a rap song and hollering about the idea of a new tax on her market income, saying, "You gonna have to talk to

A High Life girl.

A naughty nude holding a drape in front of her.

Above: A partially nude woman wearing tassels.

Right: A young woman wearing a grass skirt in the doorway of a bamboo hut.

A young woman wearing horns
and holding a trident over a kettle.

Hi Fructose about that." Fructose, Wood's business manager [illegible]
the idea, citing a possible increase in competition that could potentially
damage his business.

Whether this reporting is true or false has not been determined; however,
an Internet search on the subject receives a number of hits.

PART V
Straight from the Horse's Mouth

STRANGE REPORTING

A June 29, 1910 newspaper article not only reported this news but also interpreted it in an unusually wicked way:

> *T.A. Johnson, pastor of the Second Baptist church of High Point, colored, was sentenced to two years in Guilford county last week upon conviction for seduction. The trial was rotten, and showed up that class of negro preachers who, instead of leading their people to higher and better things, drag them down and prey on them. The right kind of negro preacher and teacher can do immeasurable good for his race; the other sort injures them a great deal.*

Apparently, 1910 news was reported in a subjective manner.

TIME CUT OF 1909

News on July 7, 1909, focused on drastic time cuts for workers in the shops at High Point. Below is one newspaper account:

> *Beginning Friday Last a cut was made in the time of the employees of the shops at High Point. Some weeks ago the hours were reduced from nine to eight and now the days are cut to five a week. The difference is a loss of*

During the Depression, many men gravitated toward town.

25 per cent in wages and is said to be on account of light business with the salesmen who carry High Point lines of goods. This party that was to have vacated when Mr. Taft was elected still holds the county in its grip. The working man, who was promised everything he wanted is now working few hours a day and yet must pay…for his flour. Everything the working man has to buy is high and his labor, the only thing he has to sell, is low. Meanwhile the Republican party is and has been in power, the tariff is high and getting higher.

So, it seems that 1909 was an extremely hard year for the workingman. The article ends with a sad truth, "If there have been harder time…it will take an old man to recall same."

HE DID NOT REMEMBER WHAT HAPPENED

In a December 27, 1967 newspaper article, Donald Lewis, a thirty-three-year-old High Point man held on first-degree murder charges, did not remember the Christmas Day shooting deaths of three people. An article entitled "Lewis Says Mind Went Blank Before Killing," reveals the following details:

> *Daniel Lewis…continues to remain silent today about the Christmas Day shooting deaths of his estranged wife, Terri Lewis, 32, Charles Robbins, 39, and O.T. Nicholson, 73.*
>
> *Police said Lewis has maintained silence about the shooting since he was advised of his rights following the incident in Nicholson's Grocery on West Fifth Avenue [Lexington].*
>
> *Officers said Lewis did not refuse to talk at all, but when asked about the shooting, he said he did not remember what had happened. He told police that he remembered coming to Lexington and driving around the store a couple of times. He said he parked at the store and got out, and remembers nothing else until he was arrested.*
>
> *Police Chief L.C. Sheets said Lewis will probably be given a preliminary hearing in Davidson County Count Wednesday or Friday of next week.*
>
> *Sarah Robbins, 10-year-old daughter of the grocery clerk, was reportedly standing outside of the store looking in the window when her father was shot.*

Having partially lost her voice three years earlier following the accidental burning and death of her four-year-old sister, little Sarah could only talk slightly above a whisper. When she saw her father shot, Sarah ran up and down the street, knocking on strangers' doors until she found someone to call the police and then her mother. It was reported that when Sarah's mother heard her speak loudly over the telephone, she could not believe her daughter's voice had returned. Unfortunately, the day after the killing, when police questioned her, Sarah again spoke in a whisper.

LITTLE CHICAGO: THE NICKNAME STUCK

Master World magazine dubbed High Point "Little Chicago," claiming it was second only to Chicago in the number of cars stolen. David Nivens, *High Point Enterprise* staff writer, reminisces about the nickname that recalls a violent past:

> *Little Chicago. Some say High Point's violent nickname died with the violence of the 1920s and 1930s. Despite the city's crime-fighting successes*

of the last 10 years, others say the name has lived through the decades to describe the city's troubled neighborhoods.

In 1921, Motor World MAGAZINE FIRST TAGGED THE CITY AS SECOND ONLY TO Chicago in the number of cars stolen in the previous year and second to the same Illinois city in crime based on population.

It did not take long for city leaders to object to the 1920s Little Chicago moniker.

"It is ridiculous that such a report has been started and it ought to be branded as false," Dr. C.S. Grayson, Mayor of High Point told The Review NEWSPAPER IN October 1921. "That statement should be corrected. Somebody will have to prove to me that High Point is the second-meanest city before I will ever admit it."

The newspaper concluded that "in his [the mayor's] contention, he is supported by not a few influential men here."

Although the crime reports were considered accurate for just one year, they have been attributed to starting the "Little Chicago" reputation. The debate may have stirred a reaction, however. The week following The Review story, downtown businessmen met to discuss employing a private police officer. In the same year, the High Point Enterprise reported that postal employees were issued Colt automatic firearms to protect themselves from "gangs of ruffians."

Through the violent 1920s and 1930s, the city was a stop along the bootleggers' route. The Prohibition era also provided opportunities for illegal liquor sales, although city ordinances outlawed saloons. The Southside became a center for bootleg liquor, bathtub gin and speakeasies. Illegal gambling persisted, and sometimes violence erupted.

Slot machines were legal and so was prize-fighting, which was regulated by an appointed commission. Throughout the decade, church groups complained about the evils of gambling machines, slot pianos, pool rooms and prizefights, the High Point Enterprise reported in the 100th anniversary edition of 1985.

The city also produced a number of "criminals of note," Forrest Cates wrote in the *High Point Enterprise*'s 1985 Progress 100 Edition. By the 1940s, the city's "tag" had spread "far and wide." By the 1950s, the city was still infamous for crime in the South Side and West End, as indicated by the following report:

There were stories of violence in the pool halls and "beer joints" that flourished in those precincts, the Rev. James Summey, a West End community leader and former pastor of English Road Baptist Church, told the U.S. Senate Judiciary Committee.

For most of the 20th century, West End had been a blue-collar neighborhood where residents labored in the nearby hosiery mills and worked in the many furniture factories.

Things changed when crack cocaine arrived on the scene. Prostitution flourished, Summey recalled. On one Sunday morning in 1997, "there were so many prostitutes walking the sidewalks around the church area that church attendees could not turn in the parking lot for the 'Johns' picking up the girls."

MOONSHINE, BOOTLEGGING AND COUNTERFEITING

According to David Nivens, staff writer for the *High Point Enterprise*, "Liquor became an important cargo for the skillful drivers who moved it, and bootlegging also contributed to part of NASCAR's legendary roots." Following are excerpts from Nivens's article:

Jimmie Lewallen of High Point started racing in the 1930s and continued after he returned from World War II. Like many drivers, he also illegally hauled moonshine while competing in races throughout the Southeast. He knew and raced with the founders of NASCAR. Lewallen began running moonshine on a motorcycle when Main Street in High Point was a two-lane dirt road.

An interesting addition to any true story is when a close relative includes reminiscences, as in the case of Lewallen's son, Gary, a retired Archdale police chief. Gary made a movie, *Red Dirt Rising*, a fictionalized account of his father's racing career. Gary Lewallen's remembrances are poignant. He got chased many times, but he never got caught. One cold night, he skidded on the street in High Point and broke a leg in two places. His favorite delivery car was a 1938 coupe with spotlights. "It threw the law off to use the same lights," he recalled. "You did not make much money back then in racing. There was more money in liquor. I knew my father made deliveries, but he did not discuss much of that with me. I had three choices, as I saw it—racing, hauling liquor or law enforcement."

L.E. "Old Man" Lisk's life as a bootlegger vivifies yet another colorful character and inventor. His careers followed many nontraditional paths:

Also known as Junior Lisk, he invented Lisk fishing lures, and his wife, Eva, ran the company that made them starting in 1954. Lisk loved telling tales about his friend and fellow moonshiners, Junior Johnson, who went on to become a NASCAR legend. Lisk last gave the High Point Enterprise *an interview in 2000 after he published an autobiography,* I Tell It Like It Used to Be. *Lisk told the* Enterprise *that he often thought of himself as a "crusader" and had few regrets about the old days.*

Lisk's 10-year career as a bootlegger earned him a 15-month prison stint in Petersburg, Va., for running whiskey through Virginia, Baltimore and Indiana in the 1940s. He used cars, airplanes and an old bread delivery truck with The Lone Ranger and Tonto painted on the side to carry cases of whiskey back to his stores in Greensboro.

Lisk was accused of printing $100,000 worth of counterfeit bills. He insisted he was framed as co-owner of the print shop that made the phony money, which was hidden under a highway bridge. That conviction sent Lisk to prison for 22 months.

When interviewed by David Nivens, Gary Lewallen summed up the philosophy of those earlier times. "It's part of the culture," Lewallen said. "Many people don't see it as wrong to make it and sell it."

ELOPEMENT INTERRUPTED BY STABBING

In a newspaper story dated October 16, 1907, the events of an interrupted elopement caused a sensation, and this is what transpired:

Mr. Albert Myers, who lives about six miles from here, and who was stabbed seriously a few days ago by Grover Proctor, is now out of danger and is recovering. It will be remembered that Proctor was eloping with the 16-year-old daughter of Mr. Myers, and that the latter objected to the match. Words were passed and as Myers was attempting to leave to avoid trouble, Proctor overtook him and stabbed him five times in the back, penetrating the lungs.

Right: A girl and her sweetheart.

Below: A farewell kiss.

Courtship.

Although Proctor was attempting to escape with a sixteen-year-old girl, he was captured near High Point before their wedding could be celebrated. He was put in jail but was released on a $250 bond. His case was scheduled to be heard the next term of criminal court.

"RUM HEADS" NOT WELCOME

A March 29, 1934 newspaper article entitled "Gibson Is Given Chance to Quit Liquor Business" details a rather strange court case:

> Byrum Gibson, High Point man whose name became nationally known recently when the United States Supreme Court used a case in which he was a defendant to wipe out the Federal liquor cases pending under the Volstead Act at the time the Eighteenth Amendment was repealed, still figures in the illegal liquor business.
>
> Gibson was before municipal court in High Point yesterday, according to a press dispatch, charged with peddling eleven gallons from his car and with having 24 gallons more at his home. Judge Teague fined him $100 and suspended a 15 months road sentence for five years, conditioned upon Gibson entering a legitimate business. If he does so he must not permit

"rum heads" to hang around or else the solicitor can order the sentence into effect.

Perhaps this was Gibson's warning and his once-in-a-lifetime chance to quit the liquor business.

Stolen Goods Found in High Point

In a March 21, 1900 newspaper report, the burglarizing of a general merchandise store is explored. This is what the article entitled "Ward's Store Burglarized" revealed:

Burglars entered Mr. J.F. Ward's general merchandise store last Thursday night. An entrance was affected by breaking out a large window pane in the rear of the building. Four pairs of paints, several pairs of shoes, shirts, neck-ties, a hat, etc. are among the missing articles. About 28 cents in money was also taken from the cash drawer.

One June Holland is suspected—in fact it is almost certain he committed the crime. As to whether or not he had accomplices is unknown. The burglar left his old hat in the store. This hat has been identified as one worn by Holland and a relative of his says he visited her home at a late hour with all the goods mentioned above in his possession, but says he claimed that he had bought them. He left town early Friday morning before daylight, going north. Sunday Chief Wilkinson went to High Point in quest of the burglar. He found a pair of shoes and a tie on a young man who says Holland gave them to him. Mr. Wilkinson, aided by others, made diligent search, but failed to find the man he was after. Holland has a number of friends of the lower class in High Point, and it is thought they are keeping him in hiding.

Mr. Jack Sink was sleeping upstairs in the store at the time the burglary was committed, but the wind and hail prevented him from hearing the breaking of the window glass.

For some unknown reason, Mr. Ward's store seemed to be a haven for thieves because this business had been broken into for the third time in nine years. Interestingly, each of the burglaries happened in the month of March.

WORTHLESS CHECK WRITING, DRUNKENNESS AND DISORDERLY CONDUCT

The date was August 8, 1929. The newspaper caption read, "High Point Lawyer Has License Revoked." Here are the details:

> *Judge Lewis E. Teague of the High Point municipal court last Friday ordered the law license of O.D. Ingram revoked for the remaining months of the year. Such an order was made after Mr. Ingram had been convicted of being drunk and disorderly and issuing a worthless check. In each case the attorney entered a plea of guilty and threw himself upon the mercy of the court.*
>
> *In addition to revoking his law license Judge Teague ordered the attorney to pay a fine of $20 for being drunk, pay the court cost and gave him a suspended sentence. Judge Teague also ordered him to pay the amount of the check involved in the worthless check case and pay the court cost.*
>
> *There was another charge against Ingram which was settled by the lawyer paying the prosecuting witness the sum of $3 which was involved in the case. The warrant charged false pretense.*

This report also indicated that Ingram, one of the youngest members of the High Point bar, had previously given the court considerable trouble because of his issuing of worthless checks, for being drunk and for displaying disorderly conduct.

BREAKING, ENTERING, LARCENY AND RECEIVING

In this December 8, 1955 newspaper article entitled "Hearing Waived by Four High Point Teenagers," details are revealed concerning four High Point teens:

> *Preliminary hearing was waved here in County Court this morning by four High Point teenagers, each charged with eight breaking and entering and larceny and receiving counts at Davidson County establishments. After the hearing, Judge L.A. Martin set bond for the boys at $4,000 each. Previously, bond had been set at $10,000 each.*
>
> *The four are Curtis Wood, Harvey Dehart, Bobbie Proctor and Harold Coble. Wood, the only one of those represented by an attorney in court this morning, is expected to be released on bond later today. The other three may*

not be able to raise the $4,000 bond which each of them must have before the doors of the Davidson County jail will swing open.

A mystery concerning the car used by the boys in the County crimes was cleared up yesterday through work of the FBI. It was determined that the car, a 1954 Plymouth, had been stolen in Miami, Fla. Two of the boys, Coble and Proctor, admitted to local officers they stole it in Miami about two weeks ago. Earlier they had stated they stole the car in High Point.

The boys have been questioned by officers from Guilford and Forsyth counties concerning recent thefts in these areas and some of the four reportedly have admitted some offenses. However, no warrants have yet been issued from those counties. It is pointed by local officers that in the event other counties do issue warrants, the youths must first be tried in this county. The cases are now docketed for the January term of Superior court here.

An interesting aside to this courtroom experience is the fact that Wood's parents were in the courtroom. The family members of the other boys were absent; however, a group of ten teenage girls, some of them crying, had come from High Point and visited with the boys in the lockup just off the courtroom. After the hearing, the boys were escorted back to their cells in the Davidson County jail, where they remained until bond was arranged.

DEPRESSION'S HARD TIMES PRODUCED STRANGE VISITORS

Hard times during Depression days brought hungry transients to Mae MacCarter's High Point Inniss Street boardinghouse. William MacCarter had always told his family never to let anyone go away hungry. One day, a man came to the door and asked to buy a biscuit for a nickel. Lucille's Aunt Edy invited him to come in, sit down at the table and eat. He did. "Do you live by yourself?" he asked.

Edy said no but then mentioned that the boarders usually left on the weekends. "Do you have a gun?" he then asked, glancing at the old gun rack on the wall."

"Yeah," Edy said, "but it's broke."

That night when everyone prepared for bed, Herman, Lucille's brother, told her, "I'm going to set up and wait until Dad comes and talk to him." Later, Herman came into the bedroom occupied by the five sisters and said, "Ya'll be quiet; there's somebody in the kitchen."

Above: Police dogs, a policeman and a thief.

Left: Moonshine man.

Beggar girl.

When he said that, all five girls, dressed only in their petticoats, tore out of their bedroom, ran down the long center hallway and bolted toward the front entrance. Just as they reached the door, they saw shadows come out of the dining room into the hallway. Again, they ran and jumped off the front porch. Herman, one step behind the girls, picked up a piece of loose curbing and hit one of the intruders in the head. The fight was on. One of the men cut Herman and another shot at him but missed. Then they ran. After William arrived home and heard of the night's bizarre events, he called the police, but the men were already gone by then and were never found.

Depression days also produced moonshine men, beggar women and drunken husbands.

AN ENEMY APPROACHES HIGH POINT

Author Robert Marks recalls an enemy "as relentless as the Hun" that "was creeping toward High Point in the form of the most contagious and deadly influenza ever known." The year was 1918, and this is what happened:

Influenza had already caused significant deaths in Europe, including over eight million in Spain, thus taking the name "Spanish Flu." It arrived in September, and town leaders moved quickly, realizing the havoc of the illness in other communities. Public assemblies were banned, affecting theaters, clubs, amusements, and even churches; but, such closings did little good, as factories and businesses remained open. Symptoms included pain in the eyes, ears, head, and back, dizziness, vomiting, blisters, nosebleeds, coughing, oppressive fever, and delirium.

According to reports, by mid-October there were over seven hundred cases, and fifteen people had died, including the mayor, W.P. Ragan. Before it was over, these numbers would more than triple.

WICKED FIRE KILLED GROOM-TO-BE—OR DID IT?

A December 21, 1933 newspaper account entitled "Victim of Fire Planned to Wed Lexington Woman" tells of a well-to-do High Point farmer, Lee H. Harvell, who burned to death at his home early on the day he was to be married to Mrs. Troy Frances Clapp. Mrs. Clapp told reporters that she and Mr. Harvell had planned to go to Danville, Virginia, marry and then return to his home for the Christmas holidays. She also told the press that Mr. Harvell, the father of several grown children, had told her "he was to receive more than $1,000 last week."

Investigations yielded the following facts:

Mr. Harvell's automobile was found backed into his garage and in it were an electric iron, pillow, sheets and clothing articles which Mrs. Clapp stated she had not understood Mr. Harvell intended bringing with him on his trip.

These statements were reported made in the course of an investigation which officers are conducting into the death of Mr. Harvell, who was burned to death in his flaming home. A number of circumstances have led to suspicion that he was murdered, with robbery as a possible motive.

Further investigation revealed that Mr. Harvell had not been paid the $1,000 before his death. Officers said they were interviewing a High Point "woman friend" of Mr. Harvell's. In addition, "indications of probable murder were added by finding blood stains on bits of clothing of the dead man and also on linoleum on which his body lay after the fire."

High Point Man Charged with Two Moral Offenses

The article's caption read: "High Point Man Faces Two Moral Charge Offenses." The date was June 19, 1956. Calvin Waggner, twenty-eight, of 507 Jennett Street, High Point, is accused "of assault with intent to commit rape on a 14-year-old Davidson County girl. In yet another case, Waggner is accused of assaulting a 13-year-old girl" from Davidson County. The preliminary hearing was set for that Friday.

White Girl Professes Love for Negro

The year was 1947. The *Beacon*'s front-page caption read: "White Girl Professes Love for Negro." Here is the story as it was reported:

A fairly presentable looking young white girl and a negro man have been arrested…for living together like man and wife while the negro man's legal wife was away. The young white girl who was working as a waitress was liberal in her talk with arresting officers about her love for the negro man and time and again declared she would marry the man were he not already married to a woman of his own race.

According to the newspaper account, the "lovely" romance began the previous fall but was ended in police court when the white girl was sentenced to a year in the state prison. Her Negro lover was given a year on the highways at hard labor.

Florence Woddle and Claude Long Jr. pledged their love for each other. Apparently, tips from Long's neighbors reported him as "practically living with the white girl without the benefit of the law of the clergy." Long's wife, though she said she knew of the affair, was afraid to report her husband and have him arrested.

When Miss Florence took the stand, the curious spectators heard a "recital as bizarre as the romance":

She said she was a native of Pennsylvania and she had been reared and trained not to make any racial distinctions. She said she had not realized there was anything wrong in her close association with Long. In fact, testified Florence, she heard inner voices speaking to her and urging her into the actions that she took. She said she called the voices that spoke to her the voices of God, but that Long called the voices the voices of Jehovah. She said that her living with Long resulted from the urgings of those voices, which Long likewise recognized, and felt were intended for them to hear.

When officers arrested the pair, they found two letters in Long's possession. The first was a letter from John Harden, secretary to Governor Cherry, informing Long that the governor had received his "request for information about the laws concerning the marriage of Indians and white women" and had forwarded that letter to the attorney general.

The second letter, from the assistant attorney general's office, included a copy of the law "forbidding the intermarriage of whites and negroes," and "any person knowingly issuing licenses for such a marriage or in any way assisting in it would be guilty of a misdemeanor."

The newspaper article concludes with the sentence: "Since Long was already married and since he is not an Indian, the two letters did not cast a great deal of light on the affair."

WIFE CATCHES HUSBAND AND HIS GIRLFRIEND

The September 13, 1951 newspaper headlines read: "Wife Catches Hubby in Hotel Room with Girl." The wife was Teddy Smith McKoin, the husband was Thomas P. McKoin and the girlfriend was not identified. According to the article, when Teddy McKoin received information that her husband was "keeping company" with another woman, she paid close attention to their whereabouts. When her hubby went to Charlotte, Teddy followed. When he checked into a hotel with his girlfriend, Teddy checked into a room next door. Listening through the walls, Teddy testified in court that she could hear and understand what Thomas said to the female, but she "did not think it proper to repeat what her husband had said because his language was not the kind of language a lady should use—especially in public."

She also admitted that she heard "noises in the other room which led her to believe her husband and the girl in the room with him were intimate."

When asked by Judge Myatt how she happened to obtain a room next to the one her husband rented in the Hotel Charlotte, Teddy McKoin responded, "You can get a bell boy to do a lot for $10.00."

Neither the husband nor his girlfriend showed up in court. Mrs. McKoin, who was seeking a divorce, told the judge and jury that her husband had been untrue on other occasions. Members of the jury agreed while still in the jury box. Mrs. McKoin was granted the divorce she sought.

PART VI
And the Beat Goes On

VIOLATING PROHIBITION LAWS AND DRUNKENNESS

According to a July 12, 1960 newspaper article entitled "Woman Arrested on Two Counts," Irene York, thirty-nine-year-old resident of 1411 Johnson Street in High Point, "was arrested on two charges by Sheriff's Department officers and charged with violating prohibition laws and drunkenness."

BREAKING AND ENTERING

Apparently, 1960 was a very busy year for law enforcement in High Point. On December 27, 1960, the following report was published under the caption, "High Point Man Charged with Entering Home":

> Police last night arrested Dan Oakley, 55-year-old High Point man, on a charge of breaking and entering after he reportedly went into a local home. Oakley also was charged with drunkenness.
> Officers said Oakley went uninvited into the home of Mary Kindley, "putting the occupants of the house in fear."

IDEALS LOST AS TENSION MOUNTS

A September 16, 1963 newspaper article explores and explains, with detail, the caption "Ideals Lost as Tension Mounts in All-American City, High Point." The specifics are as follows:

> *The bustling furniture and textile center of High Point has become a confused and frightened city.*
>
> *High Point is a good, progressive and civic-minded city of 65,000 population in North Carolina's industrial Piedmont. It has been called the "Dynamo of the Piedmont," and displays the red, white and blue shield of an "All American City."*
>
> *It bears no resemblance to a sleepy farm town of the rural South. Instead High Point enjoys a booming, healthy economy and outstanding leadership.*
>
> *It has a good record in promoting racial harmony and good will. But now, somehow, apparently through no fault of the city's, that record is being blackened.*

The tone of the report then shifted from praise, harmony and civic-mindedness to a section with the subtitle, "CHANGED," which follows here:

> *High Point is a city with comparatively little racial discrimination—as near an "open" city so far as segregation is concerned as there is in North Carolina, perhaps in the South.*
>
> *It was one of the first cities to have a working bi-racial, committee. A High Point native and resident, former diplomat, editor and state adjutant general Capus Waynick is the state's top racial mediator and troubleshooter.*
>
> *High Point embarked on a policy for handling racial problems in a manner that promised to secure a model for harmony and peaceful solutions.*
>
> *Suddenly, this progress went into reverse and deep trouble has come to High Point. No one seems to know exactly why.*

The next section, entitled "STRAINED," supplies further information, as demonstrated here:

> *The city now has become one with strained racial relations and a tense racial situation.*
>
> *Last week High Point was a virtual racial powder keg. The situation was ugly and on the verge of violence. It was the principal racial trouble spot in the state.*

Nightly marches by hundreds of Negro demonstrators continued in the face of mounting tension. Reinforced police had to rush in on repeated occasions to break up clashes between white and Negros. Rocks, eggs, and tomatoes were thrown. Crowds of jeering whites grew larger. Police arrested troublemakers and many were jailed in the interest of safety and preserving order. Tear gas had to be used to separate the crowds.

The final section of the news article is entitled "DEMONSTRATIONS" and is written as follows:

The role of Negro demonstrators led by the Rev. B. Elton Cox, field representative of the Congress of Racial Equality (CORE) apparently is complete, total integration in High Point.

Cox is a resident of High Point and believes that his home city can achieve a total integration breakthrough by use of the CORE-sponsored demonstration-picketing methods.

The targets of the demonstration have been a movie theater, a drive-in-restaurant and one or two other establishments which remain segregated. These are located in an area of several blocks along the city's principal thorough-fare, in the downtown business district.

The establishments are resisting the pressures of demonstrators…

Cox and his group rejected the proposed ordinances and said they would be unacceptable. Mayor Floyd Mehan told the Council, however, that the situation had "hit an impasse" and that the attitude of the community had changed.

Mehan deplored the deteriorating situation and absence of what he called "the common sense" factor in the mass protests. He said the city had hesitated about enacting restrictions and strong control measures and hoped instead for a "cooling off" period, during which negotiations might be resumed. Church groups complained about the evils of gambling machines, slot pianos, pool rooms and prizefights, the High Point Enterprise *reported in the 100th anniversary edition of 1985.*

By the 1950s, the city was still infamous for crime in the South Side and West End.

LOTTERY ROUNDUP

Lotteries have not always been legal. In a newspaper article dated October 26, 1933, the caption read, "Judge Shaw Raps Lottery Operation":

Ernest Harris, of High Point, one of three defendants charged with operating a lottery in that city recently, plead guilty to the charges here Monday before Judge T.J. Shaw in superior court and was sentenced to six months on the road, $500 fine, and costs.

James J. Pittman and Ernest Jett, both of High Point, also plead guilty on the same charges, but sentences were withheld.

The three men were recently arrested in a "lottery roundup" by police of High Point.

STOLE HIS CHILD

The March 26, 1902 newspaper article entitled "Stole His Child" is billed as "an exciting little episode." Exciting, maybe; wicked, no doubt. This is what transpired:

An exciting little episode took place near the Nation Hotel formerly known as the Commercial, yesterday. It seems that a Mrs. Watkins, of High Point, concluded about a week ago to leave her husband. She did so, taking with her their only child, a little girl about five years of age. Watkins, with the aid of the police, located Mrs. Watkins at the National. After ineffectually trying to secure his child, Watkins came down yesterday himself. Securing a horse and buggy he placed it near the hotel and then set about to get the child. He was not long in getting hold of it and then he made for the buggy, but Mrs. Watkins was not idle and when he reached the buggy she was there also and she snatched the child away from him before he knew what she was doing and carried it back into the hotel.

The husband finally returned to High Point alone. He does not want his wife, but it is the child he is after and there will likely be other proceedings soon. What caused Mrs. Watkins to desert her husband is not known.

INJUSTICE OF CHILD LABOR

Pickett Cotton Mill was organized in High Point in 1910. According to records, "The mill produced broad print cloths and other cotton goods."

Lewis Hine took pictures in North Carolina of children working in textile mills. His work is documented as follows:

It was 1908 and Hine quit teaching, picked up his bulky Graflex, and went to work for the National Child Labor Committee; his job was to document the appalling working conditions of children across the United States. That same year he began visiting North Carolina's textile mills, where about a quarter of the work force were children under 16, some as young as 6. The hope was to produce such proof that national laws would be passed to protect children from what was in essence slavery. Some laws were in place—no child should work before the age of 13; every child must go to school at least three months a year—but the laws were not monitored, and in the South the farm family, looking for a better life, moved where the mills were.

Some of the workers in the Pickett Cotton Mill, High Point.

Children in the "Kindergarten Factory," run by the High Point and Piedmont Hosiery Mills.

Luther Purdue, nine years old, working in the High Point Hosiery Mill.

In the mill town they received steady pay, enough to eat, housing and a community of people just like them. There were problems, however, which amounted to a new kind of servitude. The children were encouraged to come to work with their mothers, and as early as 4 were

Above: Ten-year-old Pearl in the weave room of the Pickett Cotton Mill in High Point.

Right: An eight-year-old child who labored.

Young girls who worked in a mill.

Young boys and girls working in a mill.

A protest against child labor.

helping sweep. By 7 or 8 they were doffers or spinners, and school came only if they were not needed at the mill. Everyone in the family worked and, at many mills, the pay was in script, which was exchanged for rent, groceries and clothing.

Lewis Hine's visual "proof" that young children were laboring in factories and mills was made part of the Hine Report, Rural Child Labor, in 1915. Occasionally, children marched in parades to protest child labor.

Too Late to Stop the Train

The January 22, 1902 newspaper carried a piece with the caption "Killed on a Cross-Tie." A special from High Point read:

Engineer Holton, whose run is between here and Asheboro, says his engine struck and killed a white man just this side of Randleman this evening while on route here. Mr. Holton saw the man sitting on the end of a cross-tie, but too late to stop his engine to save his life. In the man's pocket was

A train engineer in his cab.

found a letter addressed to James Teague, and also a bottle of whiskey. He
was undoubtedly under the influence of drink.

ASSAULT WITH A DEADLY WEAPON

One newspaper caption dated December 27, 1957, read: "High Point Negro
Shoots Woman in the Leg." This is what happened:

> *Lou Ella McIntosh, Negro woman of 304 Railroad Street, was shot*
> *in the leg here last night, and police soon afterwards arrested Wilford*
> *Lacy McMillian, 21-year-old Negro of High Point, for assault with*
> *a deadly weapon.*

Lou Ella was taken to the hospital for treatment of the wound, and it was
reported that the injury was not serious.

MOLESTATION IN LOCAL THEATER

Carl VonCannon was arrested and tried in High Point. The charges were indecent exposure, intimidation of a witness for the state and speeding. Judge Don C. MacRae, presiding at the trial, gave VonCannon a total of twenty months on the roads at hard labor. The judge's comments termed VonCannon's activities in the local theater "the commonest and most damnable thing I have ever heard, and I've been judge of this court for a long time." Then Judge MacRae told VonCannon's attorney that "he could not tell him in open court what he though of Carl VonCannon, but when court is over I'll be glad to take you in my office and tell you how common and how low down I think the defendant really is." This is what happened to make Judge MacRae speak that way:

> *Mrs. Pearl Watson testified she was in the Carolina Theater when Carl VonCannon took a seat in the theater by her side. The woman said that VonCannon, soon as he took his seat, began to molest her and that she moved into another seat in the show house. The woman said immediately after she moved to another seat in the theater she was followed by VonCannon who continued to molest her.*
>
> *Mrs. Watson told the court that she moved her seat several times, and that each time she moved from one seat to another, she was followed by VonCannon, who continued to molest her.*
>
> *The woman also testified she started to leave the theater because she could not get away from VonCannon, but just as she started to make her exit, she was stopped by a police officer who told her he had been standing in the rear of the theater and had observed VonCannon follow her from one seat to another in the show house. The officer, she testified, then arrested VonCannon.*

VonCannon, after being released under bond, allegedly visited Mrs. Watson and offered to pay her a cash sum if she would not appear in court as a witness against him. Mrs. Watson shared these details in court.

Clerk of court M.W. Nash then informed the judge that VonCannon was wanted on a speeding charge. The judge ordered VonCannon to serve six months on the roads at hard labor and one year on the roads at hard labor when he was convicted of indecent exposure—for a total of eighteen months. Then, Judge MacRae sentenced VonCannon to two months on the speeding count—now making a total of twenty months on the roads at hard labor.

Mr. McAnally, representing VonCannon, "made a powerful plea, telling the court that his client was not a criminal but " a man who needs medical attention." The plea did not impress the judge.

PART VII
The *Beacon* Tells It Like It Is

Note: A weekly newspaper called the Beacon *was printed and distributed for five cents a copy in High Point beginning in 1941. Some of the old copies still remain. I was unaware of this publication until I visited with an eighty-eight-year-old gentlemen to learn more about the history of High Point. About twenty minutes into our talk about this book, the interviewee said to me, "You need to find some old copies of the* Beacon. *That's where you'll find your wicked events." And so I did. This chapter is devoted entirely to columns from that newspaper.*

HE FOUND HOUSE ROBBERY EASY

In the Thursday, January 2, 1941 issue of the *Beacon*, a front-page story entitled "Local Thefts Solved: Earl Williams Tells Interesting Story of How He Started on Criminal Career and How Easy It Is to Steal," Williams was described as looking more like a bank president than a thief, but he finally admitted he had committed more than 150 robberies, including many in High Point. A well-dressed man in his mid-thirties or late forties, he said that at one time he and his brother had been in business together, but he decided he could expand his wealth by stealing. In fact, he stated he had no trouble at all entering homes. Later, he informed police of the location of some of the loot. Upon investigation, law enforcement officers found much of the stolen merchandise.

DID HE TRY TO LURE MARRIED WOMAN AWAY FROM HER HUSBAND?

An article with the caption "Burton Denies He Lured Young Woman" appeared in the January 9, 1941 paper. R. Allen Burton of High Point, president of the Burton Upholstery Company and the Johnson Frame Company, filed an answer to a $25,000 lawsuit against him brought by Eugene Riddle. He denied "that tropical breezes and a Miami moon ever caused him to lure the love of another man's wife." Mr. Riddle charged in the suit that "Mr. Burton stole the love of his wife while they were vacationing in Florida. Mr. Burton lavished gifts on her and asked her to divorce her husband." Mr. Burton denied all charges and said their meeting in Florida was "incidental and casual." He also denied giving Mrs. Riddle any gifts or trying to persuade her to divorce her husband.

HE WAS THERE, BUT HE DID NOT SHOOT HER

"Farlow Tells About Argument with Wife but Denies Killing: Held for Murder," read the caption for a front-page *Beacon* article on January 16, 1941. The entire piece is composed of a conservation between the *Beacon* reporter and the jailed Mr. Farlow. Following is their reported conversation:

> *"The Last time I saw her she was holding out both arms and screaming, 'Don't shoot!' I ran by her on my way out of the house. I did not want to be caught there," said Oliver S. Farlow, held on charges of murdering his estranged wife, Mrs. Jessie Cox Farlow, killed in her apartment at 516 White Oak Street about 9:00 Monday night.*
>
> *"What made you kill your wife?" Farlow was asked as he sat on the side of his cot in his jail cell.*
>
> *"I did not kill her."*
>
> *"You were there at the time of the shooting. You admit that, don't you?"*
>
> *"Yes, I was there, but I did not shoot her. I'll tell you about it, but before I do, tell me who you are."*
>
> *"I'm a newspaper man with the* Beacon.*"*
>
> *"Are you going to print what I tell you?"*
>
> *"Sure."*
>
> *"We had been having lots of trouble from the time we were married about two years ago. She was a high tempered woman. Nobody could get*

along with her. She was mean. I tried to get along with her. I couldn't. She was just mean. I went around to see her about some bills. She flew into a fit. We argued some. All at once I heard some shooting. She was standing near the stairsteps [sic]. I started to run to her. She held out both arms and said, 'Don't shoot.' Whoever it was kept on shooting. That's all I know. I don't know who did it."

He's *My* Man

This story made page eleven on January 16, 1941. Entitled "Annie Married the Only Good Man But He Done Gone Bad," the opening line read, "Annie may be little but Annie sho' is loud." It seems that a couple of policemen cruising High Point received a radio message to go to Moon Town, where Annie Long lived. When they arrived at Annie's house, she was outside "using profanity as few people can sling it. She was actually inventing new words." Following is the *Beacon*'s report of what happened next:

> *"Look here," said Annie, "that nigger can't do me that way. I see'd him and her pass right by my door. He's my man and that gal knows we is all married up together. Jest de' same she keeps right on running 'round wid' him." According to the report, Annie resumed her screaming.*
>
> *"We don't want to lock you up, Annie. You settle down…there are other good men."*
>
> *"Good man; my goodness, mister, dat's the only good man dare was left and I married him."*

Annie then went back into her house, and "the coppers drove away."

Noble Deed to Avert Scandal

An old Chinese proverb states, "No Good Deed Goes Unpunished." The February 17, 1941 edition of the *Beacon* reported a story that might well illustrate this old saying. The piece was entitled "College Couple Wed but Boy 'Kicked Out' of School Next Day." The most unusual events unfolded:

> *There's a young man in High Point whose friends are seeking legal advice for him and contend he did a noble act to avert a scandal at a local college.*

A young woman student at the institution told college authorities recently that she was an expectant mother and that another student at the college was her "lover."

The article goes on to explain how officials at the college called the young man into their office. When the young man denied any and all charges, he was "persuaded to wed the young woman and thereby avert any possible disgrace to his school." This he agreed to do, so the next day the young man and woman, along with two teachers from the college and the bride-to-be's father, made a "quick trip" to South Carolina, where the couple "became man and wife."

Now, all was still not well. When the bridal couple returned to High Point, the groom was told, in no uncertain terms, that he must quit school. According to the *Beacon* article, the young man was extremely disappointed in college authorities because he had "performed a noble deed to save his school from any criticism."

Madam Maza's Sudden Departure

Apparently, Madam Maza was a fortuneteller who departed High Point after giving glowing readings to a High Point woman. In the May 1, 1941 issue of the *Beacon*, an article entitled "Madam Maza Disappoints Women by Sudden Departure" gave the sordid account of the madam's ventures in High Point. The teaser read, "Madam Maza is gone and the F.B.I. boys are hot on her trail." It seems she left before some of her glorious predictions came true for the town's women. Madam Maza apparently gave some mighty fine romantic readings:

H. Pointer is awaiting the return of Madam Maza because she firmly believes when Madam Maza returns to her home, she will be accompanied by a tall, dark complexioned young man who will offer to marry the High Point woman.

In addition to being handsome, the tall, dark, and handsome man will be very wealthy and will take his bride on a tour to the West Coast and show her all about the motion picture industry. For all this information and hope, the High Point woman paid Madam Maza the neat sum of $750.

The conclusion of the article was a business plea. The publisher of the *Beacon* asked for a tip on Madam Maza's present address because she "forgot to pay for her ad before she left town."

MAYBE HE'D BETTER PASS ON THE DRINKS

The May 8, 1941 edition of the *Beacon* included a hilarious story with the caption "High Point Salesman Gets in Trouble by Visiting for Drink." It seems that the High Point gentlemen on whom this story was based traveled regularly. This article was about a trip he made to a far-distant city. The sequence of events concerned a young female passenger, cocktails and dinner, followed by a trip to the parlor car for more drinks. At bedtime, the High Point traveler and the lady separated; each went to his or her separate car. The High Point native put on his pajamas and then wove his way through several cars, drank some more and went back to his designated car. He found that every berth had been filled with sleeping travelers, so he went to the porter, asking where his berth was. The porter said, "My goodness, Captain, you are supposed to be on another train. Your car was switched an hour ago to the westbound train. Your car is at least fifty miles from here."

The sot's coat of arms.

The conductor was called in, and he immediately found the High Point fellow a berth. Without his luggage or money, the gentleman was stuck, so he decided to get off the train the next morning. Soon after, he sent a collect telegram to High Point for funds to return home.

DRAGGING WIFE AND HITTING HUSBAND WITH WHEELBARROW

One of the strangest wicked incidents in High Point was reported on July 10, 1941, by the *Beacon*. The title of the piece was "Dragging Woman by Her Ears Is More than She Can Stand" and concerned Mrs. T.L. Wilson, who testified against her husband in a charge of assault. The courtroom testimony was as follows:

> *Well, your honor, I was in the kitchen ironing some pants for my husband to wear when he comes in and asked me if I love him. I tells him I don't and he slaps h--- out of me. Then he throws me down and tries to smother me. He nearly did a good job of it. Then I gets up and he knocks me down again. Then I start to call for help and he slaps me down again. Then I tells him I do love him, but he keeps on beating me.*
>
> *Then he knocks me down again and catches me by both ears and drags me into the bedroom.*

T.L. Wilson testified and admitted that he did drag his wife around, but first his wife had tried to hit him with a wheelbarrow. The judge intervened for clarification concerning the wheelbarrow and discovered from Wilson's next words that it was a toy wheelbarrow. Wilson did not relent. "It was a toy wheelbarrow and she could knock the devil out of me with it, but I would not let her. I knocked her down. I smothered her to keep neighbors from hearing her yell so loud."

Spectators "literally rocked the building with laughter," and Judge MacRae sentenced Wilson to two years on the county roads but suspended the sentence on the condition that he not abuse his wife again and not appear in court for two years.

Coach Charged with Duplicity

High Point College charged Jim Mallory, Elon College football coach, with "duplicity" because High Point College athletic authorities said he "backed out on a verbal agreement to accept the position of football coach and director of athletics at High Point College." A newspaper article dated February 1, 1950, with the caption "Jim Mallory Is Rebuked by High Point Officials," related the details behind the charge: "Dr. Dennis Cooke, president of High Point college, denounced Mallory today for what the president termed, 'The most outrageous conduct I have ever encountered.'"

Dr. Cooke said Mallory was offered the High Point job and the opportunity to name his assistants. He chose Carroll Bowen, coach at High Point High School. Mr. Bowen accepted the offer and resigned from the school system. In addition, Dr. Cooke related that after Mallory accepted the position, he wired all other leading candidates to let them know the vacancy had been filled.

High Point Man Suspected of Break-Ins

The date of the newspaper report was August 26, 1951. The caption read, "Escaped Negro Prisoner Held in Thomasville." The subject was a High Point African American man suspected of breaking into four automobile dealerships and taking over $1,000 from one safe. His name was Garland McGreger, age thirty-one, and he was suspected of working with another Guilford County man, who broke out of the Guilford County jail. And that's not all. The saga continued:

> *The High Point man is also wanted in connection with two other break-ins staged several months ago. In court here tomorrow he will be given hearings on six charges of breaking, entering, larceny and receiving.*
>
> *Sgt. Henry Easley and Deputy Dock Lee of High Point returned McGreger to Thomasville last night from Camden. After his hearing here, McGreger will be taken to the Guilford jail to resume his wait for Guilford Superior Court trial on five robbery counts.*
>
> *While McGregor was being returned to Thomasville yesterday…Chief Shore signed four breaking, entering, larceny and receiving warrants against McGreger for allegedly breaking into Paul Motor Company, National Motor Company, Collins Auto Supply and Lawing and Welborn, all located in the same block on the national highway.*

The conclusion of the article revealed the statement: "The High Pointer is believed to have taken $1,022 from the Paul Motor safe, between $5 and $6 from the Colliins safe, and to have forced his way into the other two concerns. Nothing was moved from National Motor and Lawing and Welborn, but officers found evidence of attempt to reach their safes."

ACCUSED RAPE AMONG THE LUMBER PILES

The Thursday, July 27, 1950 front page of the *Beacon* carried a bold caption: "Accused Rapist Caught." According to the newspaper column, Dolph M. Snider was arrested for attempting to rape a fifteen-year-old girl:

> *Snider is charged with attempting to rape Jacqueline Grissom, of 413 Kearns street. The crime is alleged to have been committed among the lumber piles at the Marsh Furniture Company plant Tuesday night about 9 o'clock. Doctors who examined the little girl immediately after she escaped from Snider said she was badly bruised but returned a medical report showing the man had been unsuccessful in his rape attempt.*

Jacqueline told officers that she was on her way home from a store in High Point, and the man stopped her and asked if he could walk her home. She allowed him to accompany her "because [she] had seen him a lot of times before around the store and thought he was all right."

Snider was placed in the High Point jail, and bond was set at $5,000, which he was unable to furnish.

OH, WHAT A TANGLED WEB WE WEAVE

One newspaper caption read: "Husband Catches Man in Wife's Bedroom." The saga grew more complicated. It seems there were *two* men sitting on the bed where Mrs. Daily Smith was lying when Mr. Smith arrived home unexpectedly. That, according to the article, caused a "big fight," and ultimately Wayne Saunders was arrested for "being drunk and disorderly, assault upon Smith and trespassing." When Saunders was tried in Municipal Court, he related that Mrs. Smith had invited him to her apartment "to take a drink," and he went—and stayed—because Mrs. Smith owed him five dollars and refused to pay. Judge Don C. MacRae asked Saunders who had invited him to the Smiths' apartment.

"V.J. Henderson invited me into the apartment to take a drink," he responded.

Then, Henderson, called to the stand, testified he had "purchased a bottle of gin from Lexie Davis and had gone to the Smith apartment to take a drink." He also said he invited Saunders to accompany him. Following is a summary of Henderson's testimony, according to the *Beacon*:

> *Henderson said after he, Mrs. Smith and Saunders had "killed" the gin he inquired about getting more whisky and Mrs. Smith told him to go back to the Davis apartment for what he wanted. He said he went and purchased a bottle of whiskey which he took back to the Smith apartment and continued the drinking "party." When the whisky was gone, he said, he did not have any more money and Saunders would not buy any more whisky.*
>
> *Henderson and Saunders told the court that Mrs. Smith suggested to Saunders that he loan her $5.00 so more whisky might be purchased. Saunders said he loaned the woman the $5.00 only after she agreed he might take clothing that belonged to her and hold it until she repaid him the $5.00 loan.*

When it was Mr. Smith's time to testify, he took the stand and explained to the court that when he arrived home about eleven o'clock on the evening in question, he found Saunders and Henderson with his wife. He immediately told both men to leave. Henderson did, but Saunders stayed, saying he wanted the five dollars Mrs. Smith owed him—or her clothing, for security.

Saunders reportedly jumped on Mr. Smith, knocked him to the floor and threatened to kill him.

When Mrs. Smith testified, she swore that she had taken only a few drinks and had not engaged in any immoral acts. She related that Saunders insisted that he receive either the five dollars or some of her clothing. In addition, she said she was afraid "Saunders would have killed her husband had she not gotten into the fight," so she helped her husband throw Saunders out of their apartment.

When Saunders took the stand, he said that Smith or his wife had knocked him unconscious and that only after officers appeared at the apartment did he regain consciousness.

After testimonies were given and evidence disclosed, the true story took an unusual twist:

> *When officers had heard all of the evidence they went to the home of Lexie and Worth Davis where they found whisky so the man and his wife*

were arrested, charged with violating the prohibition law. During the trial yesterday Prosecuting Attorney Louis Fisher ordered a bench warrant issued for the Davis man and woman and told officers to charge them, in a second warrant, with violating the prohibition law "because these people say they purchased whisky from both Mr. and Mrs. Davis."

FORMER PREACHER IN TROUBLE AGAIN

The front page of the Thursday, July 27, 1950 edition of the *Banner* presented one "wicked" High Point true story after another. One article, entitled "Husband Chases Preacher," probably drew residents' interest. The lead paragraph stated, "There's a long story 'behind the story' of the trial of W.M. Bell who was convicted this week of abandonment and non-support of his wife."

Apparently, this was not Bell's first appearance in court, as indicated by the following printed information:

> *The former preacher was convicted some time ago of a serious crime and when his wife got him into court this week for abandonment and non-support he found the going mighty rough. When Judge Don C. MacRae passed sentence upon the former minister he immediately appealed the judgment to the superior court so his wife will have to tell her story to a jury now before she gets any financial help from her husband. Judge MacRae ordered the man to pay his wife $60.00 immediately and then pay her $20.00 each week in the future. It has been learned that Bell is responsible for two High Point children being in a boarding home today. A prominent High Pointer says the man "stole" his wife from him and he found it advisable to put his children in a boarding school.*
>
> *The man in question says he has tried, time and again, to kill the former minister but each attempt has failed. He says only a short time ago he found the former minister and his wife together in an eating place…and when Bell saw him he ran and called deputies to come to his rescue.*

The unnamed man also told a *Beacon* reporter that once he ran into Bell in a High Point garage and tried to catch him so that he could "cut his throat," but the former minister got away.

"The reason he can't care for his own wife is because he is too busy caring for other married women," said the man in question, "but I'm mighty glad his wife has finally found out what it's all about and has taken him into court."

Twenty Shots Extracted from His "Seat"

A newspaper caption read, "Preacher's Son Is Shot." The date was July 27, 1950, and the source was the *Beacon*. The lead paragraph stated, "Two brothers—sons of a well-known preacher—are scheduled to be tried this week for breaking, entering and larceny." The second paragraph began, "But that's not half of the story. What actually happened during the alleged larceny is what makes a good story but what happened caused Charles Manuel to seek a doctor who extracted about 20 shot from his 'seat.'"

Following is the other half of the story:

> *Several nights ago Moody Dunn, saw mill owner and operator, returned to his tent to find thieves had visited while he was away and some of his valuables were missing. Mr. Dunn, by a "hunch," decided the thieves might return to his tent on Saturday night so he hid and waited.*
>
> *The saw mill owner and operator had not been in hiding long before he saw the two Manuel brothers approaching. Mr. Dunn lay quiet for a while. He saw the two brothers peep into his tent several times. Then he watched them as they surveyed surroundings.*

Then the boys went into the tent and started gathering up more items. As they left, Dunn shouted for them to stop, but according to the report, the boys "lit out." Dunn aimed at their backs, and birdshot flew from his gun into the backside of one of the boys, Charles. That stopped the two boys, and they surrendered to Mr. Dunn, who marched them to deputies. This true story ends with a doctor picking the birdshot out of Charles's "behind" before he and his brother were jailed.

He Picks on Child by First Husband

A front-page extra in the July 27, 1950 *Beacon* was entitled "Stepson Causes Trouble." It seems that Mrs. R.C. Johnson of High Point appeared in court and announced that the only trouble she ever had with her husband was "because of a child by her first marriage." Mrs. Johnson told the court that other than "always picking on my child by my first husband," Mr. Johnson provided well for her and was a good husband.

According to the newspaper report, a reportedly frail Mrs. Johnson sobbed while in the witness chair as she related her husband's anger, which resulted in his beating her son. In addition, she said if she interfered, her husband hit her; therefore, she signed a warrant against him, charging him with assault. "He actually foams at the mouth," Mrs. Johnson told Judge MacRae.

Mr. Johnson denied the charges, and he told the court that his wife only wanted to get a court record against him. He did admit that "he felt since he provided for her son...he should have the right to discipline the boy." In addition, Johnson testified that his mother used a leather belt to beat her son.

What was Judge MacRae's ruling? He sentenced Johnson to a long term on the roads at hard labor but suspended the sentence "providing he would adequately support his wife, not assault her or her boy again, and be of general good behavior."

So what did Mr. Johnson do? According to the newspaper article, he appealed the judge's sentence so his wife would have to tell her story to a jury in Superior Court.

HUSBAND OF TWO MONTHS HATES WIFE

According to another front-page article in the July 27, 1950 *Beacon*, Carmie Lee Presswood and W.E. Presswood appeared in court. Mrs. Presswood was asking for a divorce with support. Here is her testimony:

> *Carmie Lee testified that her husband induced her to come to High Point from California so that he and she might wed but since she married W.E. Presswood, well-to-do groceryman, he has treated her cold and cruelly.*
>
> *It was only two months ago that she and the local grocery man married but he has treated her so badly, she says, she can no longer live with him.*
>
> *Mrs. Presswood contends she worked with her husband in his Lowe Avenue grocery store and did all she could to make him a good wife but in return for all she did her husband has made life miserable for her.*
>
> *The woman charges that when she took groceries home from his store to cook for him he complained and when she ate ice cream or confectioneries while working in the store her husband would complain.*

During her testimony, Mrs. Presswood told the court that Mr. Presswood would not even speak to her unless she asked him a direct question, and then he would give her the shortest answer possible. In addition, Mrs. Presswood testified that her husband had never bought her any new clothes, had forced her to buy her own groceries and refused her any spending money. Her complaint also included the contents of a letter that Mr. Presswood wrote to her, informing her in no uncertain terms that he not only did not love her but also "hated her worse every day" and was more than ready to send her back to California.

Mrs. Presswood's testimony continued as she told the court of the tiny bedroom she was told to stay in and not venture into any other part of the house. That room had no screens on the windows and was inadequately furnished. In addition, she stated that her husband's son, daughter-in-law and two children also resided in the home. She swore she had been abused by the entire family. The saga continued as Mrs. Presswood concluded her testimony, offering the following information:

> On June 10, of this year, says the woman in her complaint, all of the furniture was moved out of her small bedroom and had she not been alert even her clothes would have been moved but she salvaged them, she says, before the dresser was finally taken from her room.

The judge's ruling was not included in the newspaper article.

DRUNK SMACKS AGED MOTHER IN FACE

According to a December 21, 1950 article, Hovie H. Wilson was jailed, accused of hitting his mother in the face. Judge Don C. MacRae "believes any man who will hit his mother in her face with his fist should not be allowed his liberty during the holidays, but should be kept behind jail bars while others enjoy holiday festivities."

Officers of the court told Judge MacRae they were not able to find Wilson's mother, Mrs. Orlia Wilson, for her testimony after signing a warrant against her son for beating her and using abusive language. They also said they thought she had fled High Point "because she is afraid of her son when he is drinking."

According to the report, Judge MacRae stated, "I think that's OK. Get her here when you can [talking to the officers]. I think this man should be kept in jail over the holidays."

ASSAULT WITH A BOTTLE OF LIQUOR

Another front-page article in the December 21, 1950 *Beacon* bore the caption "Husband Accuses Wife of Running Around with 'Lover'" and related court conversations between the judge and Tony Anthony concerning Anthony's attack on Charles Stacey with a bottle of liquor:

> *"Do you mean to tell this court that your wife has been stepping out on you?" inquired Judge Don C. MacRae.*
> *"That's right," replied Tony.*
> *"Is your wife in the courtroom now," asked Judge MacRae.*
> *"Yes, she is," said Tony.*
> *"You are telling this court that your wife is 'running around' and she is sitting here in court to hear all you have to say about her. Is that correct?" demanded Judge MacRae.*
> *"That's correct," replied Tony.*

Judge MacRae asked no more questions but issued the following statement:

> *"If your wife is running around or stepping out on you there is a legal way for you to settle the matter. You have no right to hit a man in the head with a bottle of whisky just because you have been told your wife is running around with the man you hit. We have criminal and civil courts where such matters may be properly handled and I'm going to punish you for trying to take the law in your own hands," said His Honor.*
> *"You have certainly not been of good behavior," said Judge MacRae, "so I'm going to invoke this 30-day suspended sentence and give you an additional three months on the roads for hitting a man in the head with a bottle of whiskey."*

The last paragraph of the article focused on Tony's reaction to Judge MacRae's verdict: "Tony did not seem too disturbed about the four months' sentence. He seemed to feel that hitting Stacey in the head with a bottle of whisky had served its purpose."

PART VIII
On the Lighter Side

CHRONIC CONSTIPATION

November 12, 1912 newspaper advertisements touted a permanent cure for chronic constipation, and the text, such as that below, left nothing to the imagination:

Although those may dispute it who have not tried it yet thousands of others, who speak from personal experience, assert that there is a permanent cure for chronic constipation. Some testify they were cured for as little as fifty cents, years ago, and that the trouble never came back on them, while others admit they took several bottles before a steady cure was brought about.

The remedy referred to is Dr. Caldwell's Syrup Pepsin. It has been on the market for over a quarter of a century and has been popularized on its merits, by one person telling another. The fact that its strongest supporters are women and elderly people—the cases most persistently constipated—makes it certain that the claims regarding it as a permanent cure for constipation have not been exaggerated.

It is not violent like cathartic pills, salts, or waters, but operates gently without griping and without shock to the system. It contains tonic properties that strengthen the stomach and bowel muscles so that in time medicines of all kinds can be dispensed with and nature is again solely relied on. Among the legions who testify to these facts are Mr. E. Carraux, 337 Ga. Ave., Atlanta, Ga. And Mrs. Lula Osborne, Seneca, S.C. and they always have a bottle of it in the house, for it is a reliable laxative for all the family from infancy to old age.

A medicine bottle.

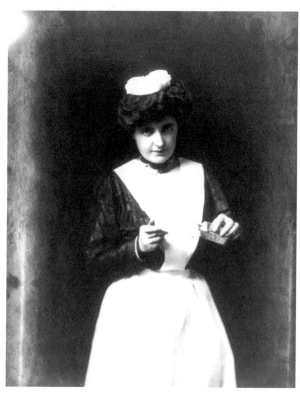

Time for medicine.

The age of drugs.

The advertisement offered anyone a trial dose before buying at the drugstore the regular size for fifty cents or the family size for one dollar. Interested parties simply needed to send their names and addresses on a postcard to the address listed in the ad.

The early part of the twentieth century was definitely a time for touting medicines.

He Was Quite a Character

A correspondent on Route 4, High Point, sent the sad news that "Old Frank is dead." Here is the obituary as it appeared in the December 8, 1909 newspaper:

> *Frank was a gray mule, and was owned by Mr. J.F. Perryman. He was quite a character and one of the landmarks of that section. He departed this life December 1, 1909, at 1:15 p.m., aged 30 years. That morning he ate a hearty breakfast and was taken sick at 9 o'clock, lingering until the time o' day mentioned. Mr. Perryman had always owned him, and Frank*

A thirty-year-old mule.

"Get along old mule."

served him well through many a season. All this fall he gave of his energy to the sowing of the wheat crop, whose straw, alas, his aged jaws will never masticate. He will be greatly missed, Frank will. His premature demise is attributed to old age.

Unique Description of Evangelists

Most newspaper descriptions of visiting evangelists in High Point were laden with traditional religious imagery, but not the one printed on January 3, 1906:

Next Friday a holiness convocation will be held in High Point and will be conducted by Thomas C.H. Hodgin and Charlie Johnson, who, it is announced are "two red hot Holy Ghost Filled Quaker evangelists."

A street evangelist.

An evangelist preaching a sermon.

NASTY RUMOR

The following "brief but powerful" paragraph appeared in the February 16, 1908 newspaper, and there can be no doubt about Mr. Cox's stand: "Mr. J. Elwood Cox of High Point not only doesn't want and won't have the republican nomination for governor, but he wants people and papers to shut up about it."

That should probably win the prize for straightforward reporting. Enough said.

WHAT DOES "IT" REFER TO?

The ambiguous pronoun "it" needs an antecedent for clarity and conciseness. Many early newspaper reports, such as this one from June 17, 1908, are prime examples:

> *Four High Point boys who passed through Kernersville one night not long ago and proceeded to let their presence be known, were arrested in High Point and taken back to Kernersville for trial, and fined $4.25 a piece. They had no idea that it was loaded and never dreamed of getting into trouble, but Kernersville went right after them.*

MIDNIGHT CURFEW WITH ONE EXCEPTION

According to author Lew Powell in his book entitled *On This Day in North Carolina*, the year 1927 saw a High Point mayoral order—with one exception:

> *Mayor H.A. Moffitt of High Point orders that all future public dances must stop at midnight. According to a dispatch in the* Charlotte Observer, *the mayor's announcement follows "a series of four terpsichorean events staged in connection with the furniture exposition. The mayor made an exception…in order that the visiting furniture men might be entertained more elaborately."*

"WE BELIEVE THERE IS DANGER"

Reporting in 1899 was quite different than it is today. On January 25, 1899, the editor of the *High Point Enterprise* wrote the following:

On the Lighter Side

Our friend Varner, editor Davidson Dispatch, *is in a bad fix; he is a single man. We have done everything in our power to help him, but without avail.*

Last Tuesday Sheriff Dorsett was in High Point and we learn that he has a standing proposition of $5.00 if the editor of the Dispatch *will marry. The* Enterprise *will supplement this amount with $2.00. We would make it more, but we believe there is danger.*

The editor of the *Davidson Dispatch* responded:

Thanks to the Sheriff and editor Farriss for the interest they feel in us and is shown by their money and otherwise, but we have never realized that a man was necessarily in a "bad fix" because he happened to be a "single man."

If all our friends would contribute as liberally as these gentlemen, the money, if nothing else, might induce some fair maiden to accept the bachelor editor. Pass around the hat, Bro. Farriss.

BOYS WILL BE BOYS!

Note: One of my long-term, interesting projects has been researching the early history of High Point College (now High Point University), established in 1924. Young students were much more formal than they are today; however, they did manage to "pull some interesting stunts." The following true stories pay tribute to those first students and their innovative practical jokes.

I had heard several versions of the "Legend of the Chapel Cow." The High Point College auditorium, located on the south end of the second floor in Roberts Hall, was the scene of the mischief. Picture rows of straight-backed chairs facing a stage where faculty members sat facing their students during chapel—a dignified, solemn, religious place and event. Usually. Picture this particular morning. Some of the young college men had borrowed a cow from Mr. Dalton across the street, coaxed her up the steps into the auditorium and obviously left her there long enough for the animal to wander and mess—and mess a great deal more. Now picture dignified Dr. Andrews, president of the college, proudly leading faculty and students to morning worship. Try to imagine his expression as he was greeted by the cow's loud "Moo!"

Mr. N.P. Yarborough, dean of men at the time, recalled the event: "Dr. Andrews was purple with anger. He dismissed the girls and questioned all the boys, who were told to stay."

Louise Adams said the entire incident was over—for the girls—as soon as Dr. Andrews saw the disorder. She admitted she probably would have missed the entire thing, except "somebody shoved me in the auditorium, so I got to see the cow." Officer Hall of Campus Security was summoned, and he organized an Official Rescue Mission to remove the cow from the auditorium. One student, Elwood Carroll, experienced a great deal of difficulty leading her from the stage, through the auditorium, back down the stairs and to the Dalton farm across the road.

In my interviews, I discovered that a cow can be led up steps without too much trouble, but getting one to go down the steps was another matter. Louise Adams recalled, "The cow was pregnant, and getting her to go downstairs was too much for her. We heard she died."

I wanted to know how Dr. Dalton reacted. Did he ask for and receive compensation for the dead cow? While visiting with Herman and Lelia Coble, I tried a new approach. "Mr. Coble," I asked, "were you responsible for that cow being in the auditorium?"

"No, ma'am. I *definitely* was not," he replied, shaking his head. "But I did help get her back to her owner."

Lelia, Herman's High Point College sweetheart and wife for more than fifty years, spoke softly, shielding the corner of her mouth with a cupped palm. "But we have a pretty good idea of who was responsible…it was…He was always playing pranks. That was a little *too much.*"

Herman calmly reminded his wife, "He's dead now, so there's no need to go into that." Then he continued, "It was Mr. Dalton's cow. I went up to the auditorium and opened the door. There stood that cow in all kinds of mess. We had to tie a sack across her head to get her down the steps and back across the road…had to blindfold her…I guess the whole think was too much for her. She was with calf and she died."

"What did Mr. Dalton do?" I asked. "How did he react to the loss of both a cow and a calf?"

"Why, he sued the college," Herman told me in a matter-of-fact tone. "Pretty steep price he asked. The cow was with calf, and the man made claim for both. The college paid up."

WICKEDLY EXCITING CLUB KILBY

It was 1927. Mrs. Ora Kilby Martin, wife of prominent High Point physician Dr. Joseph Alfred Martin, built a two-story building attached to the existing three-story hotel on East Washington Street in High Point. The addition became Club Kilby. How celebrities such as Nat King Cole, Billy Eckstein, Ella Fitzgerald and Duke Ellington came to play at Club Kilby provides an interesting dimension to the family's history.

As a young girl, Marion Martin, daughter of Dr. Joseph and Ora Kilby Martin, attended Palmer Institute, an exclusive boarding school for black females founded in 1902 by Dr. Charlotte Hawkins Brown. Located in Sedalia, a small town near Greensboro, the institute originally promoted industrial training, but in the 1930s, it changed to a respected preparatory school, stressing academic and cultural education for young African American girls. The story goes that Marion and one of her classmates, Maria Hawkins, the niece of Palmer's founder and, interestingly, the future second wife of Nat King Cole, bonded in a lasting friendship. The two young women stayed in touch after graduation, and ultimately Marion, who now managed Club Kilby, invited Maria's husband, Nat King Cole, to perform there.

This African American nightspot soon became a favorite Saturday night hangout for adults. Patrons visited the downstairs bar before going up the wooden steps to dance and enjoy musical magic. Imagine Nat King Cole, who played only in clubs welcoming black people, crooning "Mona Lisa" or "When I Fall in Love" for the eager crowd. Club Kilby rafters probably shook as Ella Fitzgerald, dubbed the "First Lady of Song," sang ballads or jazz in her flexible and wide-ranging voice. "Love and Kisses" would have brought clubbers to their feet.

To add to the famous list of entertainers, Edward "Duke" Ellington and his top-notch band offered favorites such as "Choo Choo Gotta Hurry Home" and "Rainy Nights Rainy Days." Billy Eckstein also added his magic to the entertainment lineup. In 1940, the Furniture City Elks Lodge Ball spotlighted "Harley Toots" and his orchestra.

Club Kilby closed in the early 1960s.

Interesting 1898 and 1900 Reporting

Sometimes, in the early years of newspaper reporting, a serious matter was reported in a casual manner, as was the case for this January 5, 1898 event:

> *Last Thursday evening Joe Jackson, of High Point, who is well known here was shot and badly wounded by another desperate character by the name of Duckworth. It was thought he would die from the effects, but is improving. Duckworth escaped.*

Then, on July 25, 1900, another casual example of reporting was captured in an article entitled "Nearly 100 Years Old":

Just outside the corporate limits of High Point lives a man who will be one hundred years old August 23rd next, and if he lives until January, 1901, he will have lived in three centuries. The name of this old landmark is Richard Green Kidd. Despite his old age and a fall which he sustained about three years ago which has kept him in doors, Mr. Kidd is feeling fairly well. His mind is clear and he says whether day or night he awaits the coming of the Lord. The Enterprise *in its issue last week printed a picture of Mr. Kidd which was taken at his home two weeks ago.*

The subject of this sketch was born in Petersburg, Va., August 23, 1790, was married twice, his second wife still living. His life record is a remarkable one.

Playful Bashing

Apparently, in 1899, High Point and neighboring town Lexington enjoyed "feeling their oats," so to speak. In a very early newspaper article entitled "West Lexington Is Allright [*sic*]," the editors of the *High Point Enterprise* and *Lexington Dispatch* locked horns in playful town bashing:

Brother Varner, of the Dispatch *has news this week from "West Lexington" which place we take it, is on the public square just back of the court house!*

Slums.

It affords The Dispatch great pleasure to inform Bro. Farris, the humorous editor of the Enterprise, that "West Lexington" is a young factory town about the size of High Point, located one mile from our beautiful and prosperous city.

No More "Somes"

The very early part of the twentieth century produced newspaper columns like "Didn't Want Any More 'Somes' of That Kind." Articles such as the following, dated February 5, 1902, were typical of on-the-lighter-side "fillers":

The teacher of a certain public school received the following letter the other day: "Sir—Will you in the future give my son easier somes to do at nites? This is what he's brought hoam for two or three nites back: 'If fore gallins of bere will fill thirty-two pint bottles, how many pints and half bottles will nine gallins of bere fill?' Well, we tried and could make nothing of it at all, and my boy cried and cried and sed he didn't dare to go back in the morning without doin it. So I had to go and buy a nine gallin keg of bere, which I could ill afford to do, and then he went and borrowed a lot of wine and brandy bottles. We filled them, and my boy put the numbers down for an answer. I don't know whether it is right or not, as we spilt some while doin it. P.S.—Please let the next some be in water, as I am not able to buy more bere."

Hard Luck

According to author Bill Cecil Fronsman in his book *Common Whites: Class and Culture in Antebellum North Carolina*, "bad luck seemed to haunt some people," as in this twentieth-century version of a "hard luck" song:

His horse dropped dead and his mule went lame
And he lost six cows in a poker game
Than a hurricane came on a summer day
And blew the house where he lived away
Then an earthquake came when that was gone
And swallowed up the land that his house stood on
Then the tax collector came around
And charged him up with the hole in the ground.

Fronsman also wrote, "Common whites projected many characteristics onto African Americans, including the assumption that they were prone to theft."

PONDERING HIGH POINT'S PAST

Extremely interesting excerpts from a speech written by Mrs. L.M.H. Reynolds and read at the Alexander Martin DAR meeting in September 1926 are posted below:

The first town ordinance, among other things, prohibited card playing, also prohibited obstructing the streets with wood piles, laid a tax on all shows, circuses, exhibitions, and Ethiopian serenades; and assessed city property a tax of one cent on one hundred dollars.

During the Civil War Northern soldiers under Stoneman burned the railroad station and hundreds of bales of cotton which were stored in a warehouse...

The most important and truly first factory of High Point was the shuttle block factory of Captain W.H. Snow, who came here from Vermont after the war. This industry was such an innovation that the farmers for ten miles around came to see the man who was such a fool as to pay money for dogwood.

PLEASE DON'T FRIGHTEN THE ENGINE

The arrival of the first train in High Point on November 22, 1855, was a big deal because most of the natives had never before seen a train. Curious spectators walked from near and far to witness this marvelous event; however, no word had been issued about the time of arrival. Consequently, folks arrived early in the village—just to be sure they didn't miss the big event. As with most wonderfully exciting events, several stories concerning the arrival of the railroad have survived to this day:

The engineer was a local man known to a great many of the crowd. He was full of fun and always up to something out of the ordinary. Just before the train came within sight of the station, where the great mass of spectators had congregated, the engineer, with a stagecoach whip in his hand, climbed upon the engine and sat astride it. As the train rounded the curve in sight of the expectant crowd, he began lashing the sides of the engine with all his might, thus ushering into High Point its first train.

Another tale, just as interesting, illustrated the playfulness of those involved with the entrance of the first train:

The crowd was gathered close to the tracks and several of the women held umbrellas over themselves. Just as the train loomed in sight a man stepped out on the track and said, "Ladies I will have to ask you to lower your umbrellas so you won't frighten the engine." The story continues that those with umbrellas raised did lower them and thus afforded the others a good laugh.

So, it seems that High Pointers could make a wickedly fun time—even at an extremely important and solemn event.

Most Unusual Divorce Complaint

One of the most unusual divorce complaints ever filed in the High Point court was a complaint in which Minnie Francis sought a divorce from William A. Francis. They were married on October 8, 1947, and separated two months later. The complaint said "that immediately after their marriage the plaintiff discovered that her husband was entirely impotent and incapable of sexual relations or cohabitation, from some malformation or organic interruption or derangement, the name or nature of which was, and still is, unknown to the plaintiff, except that it utterly prevented all sexual cohabitation." The complaint solemnly concluded with the statement: "No children have been born to this marriage."

Tit for Tat

According to a September 23, 1948 newspaper article, a white whiskey seller and colored buyer were in deep trouble, as they were exchanging booze for whiskey when the cops drove up in front of 1306 Furlough Street at just the wrong time:

The cops drove up in front of 1306 Furlough Street last night just at the wrong time—this is—wrong time so far as T.H. Tucker, white, and Guilford Marshall, colored, are concerned. As the cops drove up in front of the Furlough Street address they found the white man delivering to the colored man a case of white whiskey—six gallons. Both men were arrested and charged with selling and buying white whisky.

Tucker's wife and small child were with him as he was caught making a "delivery," and his car was held pending court action.

KIDS' PRANK SENDS COPS AND AMBULANCE

The scene of the July 1947 "accident" was at the intersection of High Point's Brookshire and Woodrow Avenues. Two police cars and an ambulance arrived at the scene to find, lying under a streetlight, what looked like a blood-covered body that had been run over and badly mangled. It turned out to be a red paint–covered dummy. This is what had happened after the entourage arrived at the scene:

Captain W.G. Friddle was the first officer to climb out of the police car. The officer was confident the dummy was a body and very bloody, so Captain Friddle approached very slowly—with his head bowed—as if in respect to the dead.

The ambulance driver and his helpers climbed out and began to make ready to remove the body to a hospital. They, like the cops, approached the limp "form" slowly because there was so much red paint, resembling blood. All knew there could not possibly be any life left in the "body."

All the time the cops and the ambulance people were creeping toward the dummy, the kids who had played the practical prank were hid nearby, laughing themselves almost sick. They were thoroughly enjoying their prank.

When the police and ambulance crew realized they had been victims of a practical joke, they laughed and left the scene—without taking the "body." The neighborhood people, looking from their windows, wondered why the mangled and bloody body was still in the street, and when they went outside to investigate, they found "a bunch of rags neatly tied together with red paint spattered on different places."

REALLY SHORT SHORTS WORN TO IMPRESS JUDGE

According to an article in the Thursday, July 31, 1947 *Beacon*, Clara Lee Medlin appeared in court wearing shorts that her "shapely legs might impress His Honor," as she put it. It seems that Clara's stepfather had signed a warrant charging Clara Lee with immoral vagrancy. When the case was called, "the pretty black-head stood before the bar of justice in her shorts" to learn that since her stepfather was not present to testify, she was allowed to go free. But her freedom was short-lived:

> *The next week the girl's mother was in court and perfectly willing and ready to testify against the girl. Clara, this time fully dressed, told the court her mother and step-father had made the statement time and again* [that] *they were not going to stop prosecuting her until she was in the county workhouse for women.*

Judge MacRae ruled that Clara Lee pay court costs. She also received a suspended sentence.

APPENDIX
Recipes Probably Served in Old High Point

Note: Many of these recipes, tried and tested, came from my High Point friends and associates. Enjoy!

EXOTIC CHICKEN SALAD

3 pounds cooked chicken, cut in chunks
1 8-ounce can of water chestnuts, sliced
1 pound seedless green grapes, use whole
2 cups slivered almonds, toasted (save $\frac{1}{2}$ cup for top)
2 or 3 cups mayonnaise
1 tablespoon curry powder
1 tablespoon soy sauce
2 tablespoons lemon juice
Lettuce
1 can (20 ounce) pineapple chunks

Combine the first 4 ingredients. Combine mayonnaise, curry powder, soy sauce and lemon juice. Toss with chicken and chill for several hours or overnight. Spoon on to beds of lettuce on individual plates. Sprinkle with pineapple and reserved almonds.

GREEN RICE

1 cup uncooked rice (cook and drain)
1 package chopped broccoli, cooked according to package directions
1 medium onion, sautéed in 1 stick butter
1 jar Cheese Whiz
1 can mushroom soup

Mix together first 3 ingredients and add Cheese Whiz and mushroom soup. Put in a casserole dish and bake at 350 degrees Fahrenheit, until bubbly.

BEEF STROGANOFF

$\frac{1}{2}$ cup minced onions
1 clove minced garlic
4 cups butter
1 pound ground beef
2 tablespoons flour
2 teaspoons salt
$\frac{1}{2}$ teaspoon pepper
8-ounce can sliced mushrooms
1 can cream of chicken soup
1 cup sour cream

Sauté onions, garlic and butter. Brown beef and add sautéed mixture, plus flour, salt and pepper. Cook uncovered for 5 minutes. Then add mushrooms and soup and cook ten minutes uncovered. Stir in sour cream and keep warm. Serve over rice.

SCOTCH CHOCOLATE CAKE

2 cups flour
2 cups sugar
1 stick butter
$\frac{1}{2}$ cup shortening
4 heaping tablespoons cocoa
1 cup water

1 teaspoon soda
½ cup buttermilk
2 eggs
1 teaspoon vanilla

Combine flour and sugar in bowl and mix well. In saucepan, add butter, shortening, cocoa and water and bring to a rapid boil. Then pour over the flour and sugar mixture. Put soda in buttermilk and add to other ingredients. Add eggs and vanilla. Mix and turn into a greased and floured 11- by 16-inch pan. Bake at 350 degrees Fahrenheit for 30 minutes.

ICING
Make icing 5 minutes before cake is done and pour hot icing over hot cake.

1 stick butter
4 tablespoons cocoa
6 tablespoons milk
1 box 4-X sugar
1 teaspoon vanilla
1 cup chopped pecans
1 cup flaked cocoanut

In a saucepan, combine butter, cocoa and milk. Bring to a boil, stirring constantly. Remove from heat and add other ingredients. Spread on hot cake.

ORANGE-CARAMEL NUT SUNDAES

3 oranges
1 cup firmly packed light brown sugar
1 tablespoon fresh orange juice
3 tablespoons unsalted butter
½ cup hazelnuts, toasted, husked and coarsely chopped

Remove orange peels with a vegetable peeler. Cut enough peel into very fine strips to measure 2 tablespoons. Transfer strips to a heavy medium saucepan. Add sugar, juice and better. Stir over medium heat until sugar dissolves. Increase heat and boil gently until reduced to 1 cup, about 15 minutes. Cool sauce to lukewarm. Cut white pith from oranges. Slice oranges into rounds and cut rounds into quarters. Scoop French vanilla ice cream into serving dishes. Drizzle sauce over it. Top with oranges and hazelnuts and serve.

RICH BISCUITS (THE *BEACON*, MAY 1, 1941)

2 cups flour
4 teaspoons baking powder
$1/2$ teaspoon salt
4 tablespoons short'ning [*sic*]
$3/4$ cup milk

Sift flour, baking powder and salt; add shortening and mix with a fork. Add milk. Turn out on a floured board and toss lightly until the outside looks smooth. Roll out 1 to 2 inches thick. Cut with a floured biscuit cutter. Place on greased pan. Bake in a hot oven for 12 minutes.

SMALL CAKES FOR AFTERNOON TEA (THE *BEACON*, MARCH 20, 1941)

NUT CUPCAKE

$1/2$ cup shortening
$1/2$ teaspoon salt
1 teaspoon vanilla
2 cups flour
1 cup sugar
4 egg yolks
2 teaspoons baking powder
$2/3$ cup milk
$1/12$ cup chopped nuts

Combine shortening, salt and vanilla. Add sugar gradually and cream until light and fluffy. Beat egg yolks until very thick and light in color and add to creamed mixture. Beat well. Sift flour and baking powder together 3 times. Add small amounts of flour to creamed mixture, alternating with milk, beating after each addition. Add nuts. Pour better into cupcake pans greased with fat. Bake in a moderate oven for 30 minutes.

ICING

Sift 2 cups confectionary sugar. Add ¼ cup cream slowly, beating well. Add any desired flavoring.

Bibliography

Beacon. "Accused Rapist Caught." July 27, 1950.

———. "Bloody Fight Over Girl Occurs in Local Diner." July 13, 1950.

———. "Drunk Smacks Aged Mother in Face." December 21, 1950.

———. "Dummy Sends Cops and Ambulance on Wild Run." July 31, 1947.

———. "Girl Without Shorts Does Not Get Very Much Mercy." July 31, 1947.

———. "Grocerman Sued Here." July 27, 1950.

———. "Hubby Beat When Wife Tells Story." January 8, 1948.

———. "Husband Accuses Wife of Running Around with Lover." December 21, 1950.

———. "Husband Catches Man in Wife's Bedroom." July 27, 1950.

———. "Husband Chases Preacher." July 27, 1950.

———. "Man Kills Wife with Hatchet and Slashes Own Throat." January 8, 1948.

———. "Mary Hopkins Murder May be Solved Today: Curtis Hopkins to Be Grilled at Death Scene." March 15, 1951.

———. "No Children in Family." September 23, 1948.

———. "Police Call Clara Cox Project Vice 'Eyesore.'" September 13, 1951.

———. "Police Jail White Man, Negro Girl Companion." December 29, 1955.

———. "Preacher's Son Is Shot." July 27, 1950.

———. "Reporters Not Allowed Investigate Slaying." January 8, 1948.

———. "Safe-Cracking Escapades." September 23, 1948.

———. "Sex Thrives at Drive-Ins." Undated microfilm. North Carolina Division of Archives and History, Raleigh, NC.

———. "Stepson Causes Trouble." July 27, 1950.

———. "White Girl Admits Her Love for Mustached Negro Man." July 31, 1947.

———. "White Girl Professes Love for Negro." July 31, 1947.

———. "White Men Found with Missing Negro Woman." September 13, 1951.

———. "White Whisky Is Seized." September 23, 1948.

———. "Wife Catches Hubby in Hotel Room with Girl." September 13, 1951.

———. "Woman Leaps to her Death from Top of Bank Building." July 31, 1947.

———. "Workers Disgusted at White Girl 'Making Love' with Negro Man." September 13, 1954.

———. "Young Man Sentenced for Molesting Girl in Theater." September 23, 1948.

Coble, Lelia Wagoner, and Herman Coble. Interview, July 13, 1987.

Crow, Jeffrey J., Paul D. Escott and Flora J. Hatley. *A History of African Americans in North Carolina*. Raleigh: Division of Archives and History, North Carolina Department of Cultural Resources, 1992.

Dispatch. "All Over the State." January 3, 1906; February 26, 1908; January 13, 1906; June 17, 1908.

———. "Boarders Walk Out At High Point Mill." September 24, 1955.

———. "Burglars at High Point. A Citizen Stricken by an Axe While in Bed—Much Feeling Aroused." June 1, 1904.

———. "Chair City Man Crashes Auto of High Point Chief." January 25, 1934.

———. "Crazy Drunk, He Burned $500." November 26, 1902.

———. "Dan Hill Killed. Former Citizen of Midway Township Killed by His Own Son at High Point." February 14, 1912.

———. "Davidson Jury Acquits Farmer in Assault Case." February 4, 1935.

———. "Didn't Want Any More 'Somes' of That Kind," February 5, 1902.

———. "Escaped Negro Prisoner Held in Thomasville." April 26, 1951.

———. "Ex-Corporal Crowell States Investigation Was 'Sneaky'" January 5, 1950.

———. "Fire at High Point. Finishing Room of the Southern Chair Company Destroyed." August 17, 1904.

———. "From Over the State." March 4, 1914.

———. "Gibson Is Given Chance To Quit Liquor Business." March 29, 1934.

———. "Girl Bride Here Held for High Point Auto Theft." December 27, 1950.

———. "Gould Shoots Attendant." November 23, 1904.

———. "Guilford Convicts Shot." May 30, 1906.

———. "Hearing Waived by Four High Point Teenagers." December 5, 1955.

———. "High Point Lawyer Has License Revoked." August 8, 1929.

———. "High Point Man Charged With Entering Home." December 27, 1960.

———. "High Point Man Faces Two Moral Charge Offenses." June 19, 1956.

———. "High Point Man Pays For Death Lexington Woman." March 13, 1947.

———. "High Point Negro Shoots Woman in the Leg." December 27, 1957.

———. "High Point News." July 7, 1909.

———. "High Point Police." August 5, 1929.

———. "Hit and Run, Manslaughter Charges Against Teacher." December 23, 1948.

———. "Ideals Lost As Tension Mounts In All-America City, High Point." September 16, 1963.

———. "Killed on a Cross-Tie." January 22, 1902.

———. "Liquor Vote Debated in High Point." March 17, 1955.

———. "Local Man Admits Series Thefts at High Point Homes." October 26, 1944.

———. "Manslaughter Sentence In Traffic Death." September 27, 1956.

———. "Mr. Myers Recovering." October 16, 1907.

———. "Nude Body of Unknown Woman Found in Empty High Point House." March 9, 1951.

———. "Number of Furs Taken Is Kept in Police File." December 13, 1960.

———. "Jim Mallory Is Rebuked by High Point Officials." February 1, 1950.

———. "Joe Jackson Killed. High Point Desperado Shot and Killed by the Chief of Police of That Town." May 18, 1904.

———. "Judge Shaw Raps Lottery Operation." October 26, 1933.

———. "Jury Convicts Shackleford of Rape in Guilford." September 24, 1949.

———. "Lewis Says Mind Went Blank Before Killings." December 27, 1967.

———. "Local Items." December 8, 1909.

———. "Man Is Held in Death of Aged Mother." November 3, 1954.

———. "Manslaughter Sentence in Traffic Death." September 27, 1956.

———. "McFarland Is Pardoned." June 14, 1905.

———. "Mental Anguish Suit: The Western Union to be Sued for 'Bulling' a Message." November 26, 1902.

———. "Miss Porter Loses Valuable Coat in Hotel Robbery." August 5, 1929.

———. "Nearly 100 Years Old." July 25, 1900.

———. "The News of the Past Week." July 28, 1909.

———. "Nude Body of Unknown Woman Found in Empty High Point House." May 9, 1951.

———. "Officers Raid Panther Quarters in High Point." February 10, 1971.

———. "Our Prospects Grow Brighter." January 25, 1899.

———. "Over the State." May 8, 1907.

———. "Over the State." June 29, 1910.

———. "A Permanent Cure for Chronic Constipation." November 20, 1912.

———. "Raleigh Kaiser Shot to Death at High Point." August 15, 1932.

———. "Rape Case Nears Jury." September 24, 1949.

———. "Scott Says Patrol Commander Is Doing Good Job." January 7, 1950.

———. "Slain Woman Is Identified; Cops Seek Durham Man." May 9, 1951.

———. "Stole His Child." May 26, 1902.

———. "Stolen Goods Are Recovered at High Point." February 4, 1935.

———. "Streeton Faces Life Imprisonment." July 23, 1949.

———. "Streeton Murder Trial Continues, Witnesses Called." July 22, 1949.

———. "Supreme Court Finds No Error. Interesting Statistics in Supreme Court Opinion." December 24, 1902.

———. "Teacher Admits Car Repair Work." December 29, 1948.

———. "This Man Knew Liquor Seller; Wouldn't Tell." December 7, 1933.

———. "A Tip to High Point." June 16, 1955.

———. Untitled notice. January 5, 1898; February 5, 1902.

———. "Victim of Fire Planned to Wed Lexington Woman." December 21, 1933.

———. "Volstead Act Is Dead in Opinion of Judge Hayes." December 7, 1933.

———. "Ward's Store Burglarized." March 21, 1900.

———. "West Lexington Is Allright [*sic*]." May 17, 1899.

———. "Wholesale Chicken Stealing." February 19, 1902.

———. "Woman Arrested on Two Counts." July 12, 1960.

Fronsman, Bill Cecil. *Common Whites: Class and Culture in Antebellum North Carolina.* N.p.: University Press of Kentucky, 1992.

Hall, Jacquelyn Dowd, James Leloudis, Robert Korstad, Mary Murphy, Lu Ann Jones and Christopher B. Daly. *Like a Family: The Making of a Southern Cotton Mill World.* New York: W.W. Norton & Company, 1987.

"Helping to End the Injustice of Child Labor." www.heraldsun.com/view/full_story/122283515/article-Helping-to-end-the-injustice.

Johnson, Paul B. "Region Has Long History of Illegal Gambling." *High Point Enterprise*, July 29, 2010.

Kent, Scott. *It Happened in North Carolina.* Helena, MT: TwoDot, 2000.

Marks, Robert. *High Point: Reflections of the Past.* N.p.: Community Communications, Inc., 1996.

Nivens, David. "Bootlegging was Big, and Gave Birth to Rise of NASCAR." *High Point Enterprise*, July 29, 2010.

———. "Little Chicago: City's Nickname Recalls Violent Past." *High Point Enterprise*, July 29, 1910.

Pickett Cotton Mill Records #4488. Southern Historical Collection, Wilson Library, University of North Carolina–Chapel Hill.

Powell, Lew. *On This Day in North Carolina.* Winston-Salem, NC: John F. Blair, Publisher, 1996.

Shipman, Roy J. *High Point: A Pictorial History.* High Point, NC: Hall Printing Company, 1983.

Sink, Alice E., and Nickie Doyal. *Boarding House Reach: North Carolina's Entrepreneurial Women.* Wilmington, NC: Dram Tree Press, 2007.

Tomlin, Jimmy. "The Lurid Details: Library Speaker Presents Program on Unseemly Events in the City's Past." *High Point Enterprise*. Available online at www.hpe.com/view/full_story/10272701/article-The-lurid-details--Library-speaker.

———. "Who Killed Mary Hopkins? Heinous Murder from 1950s Remains Unsolved." *High Point Enterprise*, July 29, 2010.

About the Author

Alice E. Sink is the published author of numerous books, short stories, articles and essays. She earned her MFA in creative writing from the University of North Carolina, Greensboro. For thirty years, she taught writing courses at High Point University in High Point, North Carolina, where she received the Meredith Clark Slane Distinguished Teaching/Service Award in 2002. The North Carolina Arts Council and the partnering arts councils of the Central Piedmont Regional Artists Hub Program awarded Sink a 2007 grant to promote her writing. She lives with her husband, Tom, and two pups, Randi and Bogey, in Kernersville and Hilton Head Island.

Visit us at
www.historypress.net